MY EXPERIENCE OF POLICE DETENTIONS IN NIGERIA AND THE UNITED KINGDOM

MY EXPERIENCE OF POLICE DETENTIONS IN NIGERIA AND THE UNITED KINGDOM

OLATUNJI OLUSANYA

MY EXPERIENCE OF POLICE DETENTIONS IN
NIGERIA AND THE UNITED KINGDOM
By Olatunji Olusanya

Copyright © 2025 by Olatunji Olusanya

Published by Baruch Publishing - 07908684207
Contact Copyright Holder at
Olatunji Olusanya
Email: tunjato45@yahoo.com
Tel: 07403 232433

All rights are reserved. No part of this publication may be reproduced, stored in a retrieval system or transmitted in any form or by any means, electronic, mechanical, photocopying, recording or otherwise, without prior permission of Olatunji Olusanya

Cover & Interior Design by Karl Hunt

ISBN 979-8-89587-691-6

CONTENTS

Preface	vii
Introduction	ix

PART ONE: MY DETENTION EXPERIENCE IN NIGERIA	1
CHAPTER ONE: Tracing the Problem	3
CHAPTER TWO: Kicking the Hornet's Nest	9
CHAPTER THREE: The Morning Trouble Called	14
CHAPTER FOUR: Waiting for My Body Search	22
CHAPTER FIVE: Welcome Party at the Cell	28
CHAPTER SIX: Survival of the Fittest	36
CHAPTER SEVEN: Behind the Scene	44
CHAPTER EIGHT: Policing and Prosecution in Nigeria	54
CHAPTER NINE: The Selection of the President for the Detainees	58

CHAPTER TEN: Equality Before the Law   68

CHAPTER ELEVEN: Wonders of Nigeria   75

CHAPTER TWELVE: My Dilemma of the New Minimum Wage
of ₦70,000   84

PART TWO: MY DETENTION EXPERIENCE IN THE UNITED KINGDOM   **89**

CHAPTER THIRTEEN: London, Here I come!   91

CHAPTER FOURTEEN: Denial of Constitutional Rights   100

CHAPTER FIFTEEN: Life in London   105

CHAPTER SIXTEEN: Relocating My Children to London   110

CHAPTER SEVENTEEN: Welcome to School   115

CHAPTER EIGHTEEN: Parenting in London as a Single Parent   123

CHAPTER NINETEEN: Police Detention in the United Kingdom   128

CHAPTER TWENTY: Hope Amid Despair   134

About the Author   140

PREFACE

This book is a product of reflection, courage, and a deep sense of responsibility. It is a personal account of an ordeal that tested my faith, resilience, and humanity, but it is also a story that transcends individual experience. It speaks to a broader reality–one that many endure in silence and despair, often without the opportunity to share their truth. My journey into the depths of the Nigerian justice system began unexpectedly, as it often does for many. What should have been a routine moment of advocacy for another–a plea for fairness for an elderly woman–unfolded into a nightmare that exposed me to the stark realities of systemic injustice. It was a period of humiliation, pain, and profound disillusionment, but also one of growth, resolve, and renewed purpose. Through these pages, I have sought to document not only my own experience but also to illuminate the failures and fractures within our systems of governance and law enforcement. The Nigerian police force, like many institutions, operates in a paradox of power and neglect–capable of enforcing authority yet often devoid of the accountability that power demands. This book offers an unfiltered glimpse into that paradox, while also juxtaposing it with the structure, order, and responsiveness I observed during my time in the United Kingdom.

Writing this book was not easy. Reliving moments of vulnerability, injustice, and frustration required emotional resilience and a willingness to confront painful truths. Yet, I chose to persevere–not for myself, but for the countless others who share similar stories but may never have the platform to tell them. I hope this work will serve as both a cautionary tale and a call to action, reminding us of the immense responsibility we have to uphold justice and protect the dignity of every human being. To those who read this book, I invite you to reflect deeply on its messages. Let it challenge your perceptions, provoke your thoughts, and, most importantly, inspire change in whatever capacity you can influence. This is not a book of anger or recrimination. It is a book of hope–a hope that we can do better as individuals, as institutions, and as a society. It is my prayer that the lessons within these pages resonate, encouraging us all to work toward a world where justice is not a privilege, but a fundamental right for all.

Olatunji Olusanya
United Kingdom
05/12/2024

INTRODUCTION

The idea of justice is often romanticised, painted with lofty ideals of fairness and equity. Yet, for many, justice is not a reality but a distant aspiration–one obscured by abuse, neglect, and systemic failure. I have lived this reality. I have experienced the cold, harsh hand of injustice and felt the weight of its consequences. This book is born from those experiences. For years, I carried the memories of my time in police detention as a private burden–a story too painful to tell yet too significant to forget. But as the years passed, I came to realise that silence only enables the cycle of oppression. By sharing my journey, I hope to give voice to the voiceless, shine a light on the dark corners of our systems, and inspire those in positions of power to embrace their responsibility to create meaningful change.

This book is not just a recounting of my personal ordeal but also a critical examination of the structures that allowed it to happen. It contrasts two systems–Nigeria's and the UK's–revealing the stark differences in accountability, respect for human dignity, and adherence to the rule of law. It exposes the human cost of negligence, corruption, and indifference, while also highlighting the resilience of the human spirit in the face of adversity. I write not with bitterness but with a sense of purpose. My story is not unique; it represents the countless lives that have been unjustly disrupted, the families torn apart, and the individuals reduced to shadows of themselves. It is a call to action–for leaders to lead with integrity, for citizens to demand justice, and for all of us to recognise the humanity we share, regardless of borders, beliefs, or social status.

As you read, I invite you to reflect on the meaning of justice in your own life and your community. Think about the systems that govern us, the responsibilities we bear toward one another, and the role we play in shaping a fairer, more compassionate world.

This is more than a book. It is a testament to resilience, a critique of injustice, and a plea for humanity. It is my hope that these pages will inspire not just understanding but also action–for without action, justice remains an empty word.

PART ONE

MY DETENTION EXPERIENCE IN NIGERIA

CHAPTER ONE

TRACING THE PROBLEM

Life, as they said, is not a bed of roses. I have to thank Almighty God for His mighty hand that allowed me to overcome life's many challenges, leaving no visible scars: no signs for my enemies to trace their mark on my life. Sometimes, problems seek people out, while on most occasions, it is people who pull the strings that bring problems upon themselves, either deliberately or unwittingly. The problems that confronted me and ensnared me were those that arose when I believed myself to be innocent, doing the right thing not for my own benefit but for the sake of humanity: being good to others or fulfilling what the Lord calls me to do in defending others' interests and protection.

That is what life is all about. Sometimes trouble will find you and may drag you down paths of trauma, where those lacking patience or a clear conscience regarding the situation could easily jump to a hasty conclusion, saying 'I knew that you will fall into the traps of the law as you are a criminal.' Wise people have long said that life is not a straightforward journey; as such, human plans may not always come to fruition as we intend, at the time we desire, or in the way we expect. The proverb 'Man proposes, but only God disposes' has proven itself accurate in every respect, extending beyond academic challenges. However, if you approach the Lord or Allah with an open mind and a heart full of faith, you should believe that your request will be granted, though the timing may lie beyond human control. Sometimes, situations arise that one neither triggered nor caused, but such challenges are simply part of the journey that every human being must traverse in life.

When someone embarks on a planned journey for important reasons, but the vehicle they are travelling in–whether privately owned or public transport–becomes involved in an accident, it may not be the fault of the driver. The accident might instead be caused by another driver's carelessness or a mechanical malfunction. Such incidents can result in fatalities or serious injuries for some passengers, which may or may not be life-threatening–outcomes that are distressing for them and their families. The driver did not intentionally cause the accident; rather, it is a misfortune that befell them, not a situation they sought or created. Trouble can emerge at any corner in human life; only those untouched by such events may fail to grasp the profound grief and devastation it inflicts on the families and friends of those involved.

The devil, or Satan–whatever name you choose to call him–is said not to have a permanent place of habitation. He is believed to roam around the world, in the air, the sea, or along the roads; he may select a person or a place to display his disruptive powers. When he knocks at your door, you cannot refuse to open it, nor can you prevent him from entering your heart. According to Biblical accounts, King David had an affair with one of his soldier's wives. Fearing that his secret would soon be exposed, causing embarrassment and diminishing his status, he sought to evade the shame and consequences of his actions. In his desperation, the devil urged him to kill the woman's husband to cover his path of wrongdoing. Fortunately, he repented, confessed his sin to the Lord, and sought forgiveness, which was granted. Saul, who later became Paul, committed numerous murders against believers and the Christian faith. Yet, he was transformed on a journey to commit more crimes and ultimately became one of the greatest Apostles, spreading the teachings of Christianity.

In conversations, when I tell my friends that Satan has no fixed abode but lives in our hearts and minds, many mock my philosophy. Yet my view on religion remains firm. God, I believe, has divided the brain in every human skull into two halves. You may interpret this division in whatever way suits your perspective, but the brain is split into equal parts from front to back. The right side of the brain encourages us to do good deeds, reminding us that the Lord records our actions for judgement day. It prompts us to be honest and to treat others as we would want God to treat us. Meanwhile, the left side of the brain urges us toward disruption, convincing us that no consequence awaits after death, and that judgement day is a mere illusion. This left-side influence drives some to take drugs, engage in drug trafficking, or manufacture them. The devil instils in them the confidence to continue down this path, pushing them to repeat these actions until the law catches up with them. At that point, the devil mocks and disowns them, denying any role in their choices and claiming he never directed them towards such acts.

As the Bible says in 1 Peter 5:8, 'Be sober, be vigilant, because your adversary the DEVIL walks about like a roaring lion, seeking whom he may devour.' (NKJV).

Therefore, it is paramount that a person thinks twice before embarking on anything that could bring disgrace or tarnish the good image of their family, which their parents have worked hard to uphold. Many people have the opportunity to steal large sums of money from their employers or resort to robbery or kidnapping. However, if they are guided by a good spirit, they will turn away from these thoughts, knowing the consequences could ruin their family's reputation or betray the trust of those who supported them in securing their job. God has given everyone a brain, though not everyone uses it wisely for the benefit of society. A notable example is a lady working as a cleaner at Murtala Muhammed International Airport. While cleaning one of the toilets, she reportedly found a purse containing thousands of US dollars. She promptly handed it over to the security team so they could locate the owner. Her honesty was widely celebrated; the Lagos State government, several large organisations, and appreciative individuals recognised her integrity, offering her substantial donations and awards. Indeed, the government honoured her with additional commendations, recognising the admirable spirit she demonstrated.

There is a saying: a good name is more valuable than gold or silver, especially when it is earned through honest means. Unfortunately, many of the values cherished by our forefathers have lost significance to the current generation. Practices such as scamming, ritual activities, gang involvement, and kidnapping have become all too common, with some even boasting about these actions publicly. Police reports and media coverage reveal that, in some cases, parents are even encouraging their children to engage in these disgraceful and harmful practices. The importance of reputation and a good family name seems to have been cast aside. Surprisingly, Nigerian politicians are often found in the front row at church services on Sundays, while their Muslim counterparts are prominent at the front of the Jumaat prayers on Fridays. How could it be possible for their heavenly records to be opened to their citizens, to see all the wrongdoings they committed against their opponents during election campaigns? Imagine them at night, moving from pastor to imam, to herbalists and ritualists in godforsaken desperation. It is hardly necessary to mention their use of gangs to harass or even kill rivals who might have an upper hand if elections were free, fair, and credible. Such an approach is not found in the dictionary or religious texts of African politicians. Finally, there is the persistent tactic of smearing opponents through a campaign of innuendo: bribing certain newspapers to publish absurd, unprovable allegations designed to unsettle voters with issues that never took place.

Sadly, law enforcement agents are complicit in failing to uphold their duties, neglecting fair and regulated procedures for wrongful arrest and detention, and denying innocent people their fundamental rights. These rights, granted by the United Nations, include freedom of movement and ownership of legitimate property. This injustice is often instigated by powerful, well-connected politicians targeting those who oppose them, particularly during election periods. Imagine a man ruling a country of over one hundred and fifty million people for more than twenty-five years continuously. Does this mean that leadership has become his birthright and that no one–regardless of education, ideology, or dynamism–can replace him? We have heard of African presidents who have so little dignity that they urinate in their clothes at official ceremonies.

In Nigeria today, people are being kidnapped from their homes, snatched from private or public transportation, and held for ransom, often demanding millions of Naira. School children in remote areas have become major targets, and their abductions serve as a source of ridicule for the government, giving kidnappers unwanted fame through media coverage, both locally and internationally. Yet, there seems to be no solution to the pressing problems facing the nation–issues like the security of citizens and their property, the provision of uninterrupted electricity to support manufacturers, and the encouragement of foreign investment. People can no longer afford to build even modest homes for themselves, as the price of cement has skyrocketed to about 18,000 Naira per bag. Industrial sites have been repurposed as mega-church auditoriums. Meanwhile, students at polytechnics and universities now drive luxury cars that their professors cannot even afford on their salaries and allowances. When you ask a man bent under a heavy load why his knees are bent, he will direct you to look at his feet. We know where the pain is, but we are not yet ready to apply the ointment needed to heal it. Who is there to blame but ourselves?

CHAPTER TWO

KICKING THE HORNET'S NEST

My trauma with law enforcement in Nigeria, particularly the Nigeria Police Force (NPF), was neither planned nor intentional. It occurred in 1982 when I moved into a new home on the outskirts of Lagos, which was under the jurisdiction of Ikeja Local Government. However, the area has since been granted its own Local Council under the recently established Local Council Development Areas, a measure aimed at expanding the number of local councils in the state. Given my upbringing and the values instilled in me–values that have shaped my social attitudes and guided my life–I have always placed a high value on the security of life and property. I was prepared to go the extra mile or do whatever was necessary to ensure that every preventable step was taken, so that neither my associates nor friends would have any cause to blame me for avoidable negligence, should an inevitable adverse situation arise.

When I moved to the area, it was remote, overgrown, and sparsely populated. As a result, there were nights when, out of the seven that made up a week, we might only manage a few hours of sleep. Night-time robberies were a daily occurrence, often happening in the dead of night. The robbers would move from street to street and house to house with impunity. According to the accounts of those few who had fallen victim, the intruders did not speak like typical Nigerians, and their gang leaders was stationed outside, keeping watch for anyone who might disrupt their operations. While their agents ransacked homes, causing panic and disturbing the peace of the residents, the robbers would take whatever they could carry. In response, we banded together, contributing funds each month, and eventually hired a local night guard. When that did not prove sufficient, we took matters into our own hands, dividing ourselves into groups to patrol the area from 11 p.m. to 5 a.m., before dispersing to prepare for work or business.

Some landlords managed to build modest homes for their families but could not afford to fence their properties, leaving them vulnerable to intruders during the day or marauders at night. The community installed iron gates at key entrances, but they could only be locked at night. It became a top priority for me to ensure my house was fenced. While fencing would not necessarily prevent robbers from entering, it could serve as an early warning system, alerting people inside the house to any suspicious activity. If someone attempted to force entry, the noise would act as an alarm, prompting residents to raise their voices, which in turn could attract the attention of neighbours.

As I got to know the neighbours better, I found myself naturally drawn to some and distant from others for reasons that felt instinctive and hard to define. One neighbour I particularly liked was Mr. Q, likely because of his proximity and smartness whenever we met, often at Landlord Association meetings. He was a printer by profession and business. His home, though modest, was well-designed, with what we would call a 'Boys Quarter' when viewed from the outside. It had a modern look. He also owned a white Beetle, which he would park in front of his house. Then, in the 1980s, it seemed unfortunate to build a house in the area without a fence. Anyone could easily cut through the property or cross from one street to another without a barrier. The Beetle, which was a popular car during that era, was one of the main targets of car thieves. Its history of theft was higher than the other models, like the Peugeot 404 and the Santana. Research suggested thieves would wait until the owner parked their car and walked away, then sneak in and drive it off using a master key. Duplicating a Beetle's key was easier than for other cars, such as the Ford, Citroën, or Skoda, which were harder to steal when parked at that time. Because of that, car thefts often involve violence, such as the thief forcing the driver to hand over the keys during traffic hold-ups or while cornering them at a quiet spot along the road.

Mr Q and I became somewhat close, and due to my personal philosophy, I offered him the use of my compound for parking his car overnight, as I only had one car in the driveway. I told him the space was at his disposal if he needed it. He said he would consider the offer, and after about five days, he began using the compound to park his car. For the next three and a half years, he parked his car there, until the gate was locked around ten o'clock in the evening, at which point he could no longer park. After that hour, he would have to park in his compound. Each time we met, he shared his business struggles with me. He explained that he had few contracts, which was affecting his financial situation. Since I was not in the same profession or industry, I could not offer any direct advice that would immediately turn his business around. However, I expressed my sincere sympathy and concern for his situation and promised to reach out to a few of my friends to see if they could offer any assistance in helping him secure contracts, particularly in printing stationery for their offices.

As I mentioned earlier, when someone shares their problem with me or if I notice that someone else is struggling–whether they recognise it as a problem or not–my nature and religious principles compel me to step in and offer help. Fortunately, I contacted someone working in the wage section of an airline, and he mentioned that if Mr Q was competent in printing, he would ask him to print some staff wage envelopes and deliver them as promised. He also said he would ask Mr Q to print the payslip envelopes for the junior staff at the airline. I facilitated the connection and thought nothing more of it. Later, I got informed that there had been a breach of agreement, particularly concerning delivery. I learned that Mr Q got paid 65% of the contract fees upfront. Rather than using the money to expedite the completion of the contract, his priority was to replace his old Beetle car with a new one. While the old car might have had unknown issues, it had never broken down in a way that would have caused trouble for the neighbours, nor had anyone ever had to push it down the street to start it, as is often the case with older cars. As the saying goes, 'one man's sweet is another man's poison,' and whether he exchanged the old car for the new one through a showroom or sold the old one to fund the new one was none of my concern, nor was it necessary for me to make any inquiries.

The issue with the contract did not directly concern me, as I was neither a beneficiary nor involved in the contract in any way. However, it concerned me that it could damage my reputation with the person who had entrusted me to introduce them to one another. The only course of action available to me was to tell Mr Q that if he failed to deliver, he might not be awarded another contract subsequently and that my words might no longer be trusted, which could affect others who might need similar assistance. How they resolved the situation between themselves was entirely their business.

CHAPTER THREE

THE MORNING TROUBLE CALLED

Trouble, we were taught in our primary school years, has no other name than disruption, disorganisation, and discomfort striking a person, family, or community in whatever form it chooses. Alternative names for trouble include devil, Satan, accident, and recklessness–forces that can drive a person from a stable mind into an unstable state. According to the teachings of the Holy Bible, Job was allowed by God to be tested by Satan. Similarly, in the Holy Quran, we learn that the pagans in Mecca attacked Prophet Muhammad (S.A.W) but miraculously vanished from their midst and reappeared in Medina, leading to the event known as the Hijrah. This demonstrates, beyond a reasonable doubt, that Satan or the devil has no permanent abode. Wherever he appears, even temporarily and suddenly, that place will never be the same again–at least for a time. Both religious texts inform us that Satan was granted a special, open-ended authority, a cheque without a specified sum, allowing him to operate with impunity anywhere and at any time. However, the comforting truth for those who believe in God and follow His commandments, whether in the

Bible or the Quran, is that they will overcome Satan's misdeeds, regardless of how deeply trouble may take root in their lives or families. If lies can dwell in a place for 20 years, it takes the truth less than 10 seconds to catch up with it and overtake it.

One morning, I was at home with my family, and my troubles arrived at my doorstep. I would not be surprised if some of my readers criticised me for disturbing the hornet's nest, as explained in the previous chapter, by pointing out that I was the cause of my troubles. Family upbringing, religious doctrines, and the values instilled in us were the fundamental principles that shaped our character and philosophy as we grew up. Although I cannot claim to have been completely oblivious to the changing tides of life, I was aware that, particularly for the newer generations, the world was evolving–and they were evolving with it. In my day, there was no such thing as child abuse, gang violence, cult membership, or senseless killings without any discernible reason. Back then, children could not report their parents to the police or social services for allegedly bullying them for failing to follow instructions or complete their chores. Today, a three-year-old in the United Kingdom can dial 999 to report that their parent has shouted at them, making them feel upset. The operator would ask for the caller's address, and within moments, the house would be visited by an unwelcome group of police officers banging loudly at the front door. What follows is a series of interrogations, with law enforcement taking the child's statement at face value, as they have been trained to regard adults as unreliable. That morning, much like the many before it, began with the usual house routines before work. Yet, without warning, it soured, and an air of mystery settled over our compound–a feeling noticeably absent in the neighbouring one. As was customary, after the children finished their breakfast, which was usually rice, their mother would get them dressed for school while I took on the supportive duty of cleaning up the dining area. This meant clearing away any food remnants that had fallen from their spoons onto the table and floor.

We kept a fair number of chickens in the compound, and one way to feed them was by tossing these scraps down the stairs as a kind of morning treat. I had noticed that our chickens seemed to have developed a routine, eagerly anticipating the leftovers from the children's breakfast. As soon as I opened the door, I would see them racing to the usual landing spots, gathering together with keen anticipation. Amusingly, they would tilt their heads sideways, studying where the crumbs would fall. It is always enlightening to observe the behaviours of those with whom you share your environment–even the animals. There is a certain charm in noticing how creatures, big and small, adapt to the rhythms of our daily lives. As I was tossing out the remnants of the children's breakfast, I paid little attention to the gate opening, assuming it was simply the downstairs neighbour heading out early. Suddenly, I spotted Mr. Q walking into the compound from one of the adjacent roads. Just as he entered, he looked at me and asked the million-pound question, 'Uncle, where is my car? I parked it here last night.', he said, pointing to a specific spot in the compound, his fingers dangling a bunch of keys. 'The keys are here with me.', he added.

My initial thought was that someone from the downstairs flat might have opened the gate early to head to work or on business. In an instant, it felt as if I had evaporated, like water on parched ground. The only response I could muster was, 'Are you sure you parked it here last night?' The only sensible option at that moment was to ask him to wait while I came downstairs. I dashed back inside, changed out of my pyjamas into something casual, and joined him in the compound. Honestly, I did not know what to say as I stood there, simply looking at him with deep sympathy. My concern was not just for the lost car but for what lay ahead–whether insured or not, Nigerian insurers were notorious for shirking their responsibilities. In times of need, they often become evasive, bombarding you with endless questions that make you regret ever trusting them. The agents are all smiles when you bring them business, but when it is time to make a claim–no matter how straightforward or valid–they will demand every bit of evidence, some of which are almost impossible to provide. At that point, the car owner had no other option but to report the missing car to the nearest police station, the Ikeja Police Station. I drove him there and dropped him nearby as I needed to report to my office, brief my staff on the incident, and obtain permission from my boss before heading back home to join any search efforts organised by the police. Within two hours, I returned home, but what I encountered outside my house was beyond my imagination.

Before I left earlier that morning, I checked with the family living downstairs. They mentioned that no one had left the flat and confirmed that the car had indeed been parked in the compound before they locked the gate. Strangely, the two padlocks used to secure the gate were gone, with not even a piece of metal left behind. It led to the theory that either the thieves had used a master key to unlock the padlocks or perhaps an electric saw to cut them, taking the remnants with them to avoid leaving evidence. I was sure there was no forced entry, as any loud noise would likely have woken me and the other residents or even alerted the neighbours. When I returned home, I found a crowd gathered outside–faces both familiar and unfamiliar, people I knew and others I did not. My first thought was that perhaps they had located the missing car, maybe abandoned somewhere, or it had broken down. However, their sombre expressions told a different story, as if a religious revival were happening in my compound. Among the crowd was Mr Q, and a landlord I knew through local landlord association meetings. Although I had heard various rumours about his past indiscretions, I chose not to judge people based on hearsay; my philosophy has always been to take people as I find them. After all, gossip often serves to demonise others. As the Bible says, 'The measure you use to judge others will be used to judge you on the day of reckoning.' Therefore, what others say about Mr A's character or lifestyle holds no sway over me. We rarely crossed paths outside those association meetings, and even then, he only occasionally attended while I served as general secretary.

As I drove into my compound, I noticed the crowd dispersing in ones and twos. No one approached me, asked questions about the incident, or cast any accusations my way. In my mind, I had allowed a sleeping dog to lie, letting peace reign undisturbed. What I later discovered about the incident, however, will be covered in future chapters of this book. My wife did relay a curious detail to me: three men had entered the compound, walked around in silence, and left without so much as a word. Although she had greeted them out of respect, they ignored her entirely, moving past as if she were invisible. Within two hours of my return, Mr. Q arrived with two young men, both dressed casually in civilian clothing. They introduced themselves as police officers from the Ikeja Police Station, assigned to investigate the theft of Mr. Q's car. Together, we went downstairs to inspect the gate, where they thoroughly examined the ground, hoping to find traces of the missing padlocks. Regrettably, the officers had no equipment for forensic analysis–no fingerprinting tools, Deoxyribonucleic Acid (DNA) testing, or any technology that might identify physical evidence like those in the crime dramas or by the Special Security Services (SSS) abroad. Such forensic services were not publicly available in Nigeria at the time, if at all. Instead, their approach was straightforward: they questioned the suspect, noting his responses in their notebooks. The suspect had no right to review his statements for accuracy; any discrepancies went unchecked. He would be asked to sign the statement as an official record. This process felt theatrical, and, like a drama, one had little control over the sequence. What could not be changed had to be endured. Cooperation was essential, for any deviation would be viewed as obstructive or uncooperative in the investigation.

The way Mr Q was looking at the policemen made it seem as though he was urging them to take all of us to the police station. Noticing his body language, I asked for a moment to speak privately with my wife. I explained that I might be taken to the station and held there indefinitely. Instead of steeling herself, my wife burst into uncontrollable tears and, as is our cultural practice in moments of hardship, began lamenting about the prolonged troubles that had beset our family. Having spoken with my wife, the older of the two policemen–likely the senior of the pair–cleared his throat and delivered the news I had feared: I would need to accompany them to the station to clarify *the grey areas* in their investigation, and he advised that I should not bring my car. That led to a three-week *holiday* behind a bar at the Ikeja police station.

Later, when I returned home from the three traumatic weeks in police detention, neighbours told me that Mr A and Mr Q, along with Mr Q's three relatives, had gathered at a nearby beer parlour the very evening I was taken away. There, Mr A reportedly urged Mr Q to ensure that I was denied freedom until I could be brought to court, regardless of how long that might take–a statement that in itself breached my human rights by insinuating I was a car thief. Ironically, I was not given the standard caution upon arrest–'You are now under arrest; anything you say may be used as evidence against you'–nor was I handcuffed. The policemen neither arrived in an official vehicle nor forcibly pushed me into a car, as you might expect in a typical arrest scenario. I distinctly recall that Mr Q paid the policemen's transport fares while I paid mine. During our journey to the station, there was no conversation between Mr Q, the policemen, and myself. It was as though we were opposing teams from different worlds, unwilling to acknowledge each other.

While the officers went to deliver the outcome of the investigation to the Divisional Police Officer (DPO), I sat in a small hall waiting for them. Upon their return, they completed their reports and informed me that I would be detained in a police cell. They explained that it was to allow them to conduct a thorough investigation without interference, assuring me it would only take a few days. Only the most gullible would believe this claim of a swift investigation, especially when I was the sole suspect in custody. I protested and requested to speak with the DPO, but my appeal was unconditionally refused. I was neither offered any legal assistance nor asked if I required the services of a lawyer. I was made to understand that I was not being formally charged in court–they just wanted to keep me out of the way to continue their investigation without hindrance. Essentially, I had no option but to face an indefinite detention, isolated from my family and work. Raising human rights issues with the Nigerian police is as reckless as pouring petrol on a fire. If you mention the Constitution or appeal to their sense of human dignity, they will quickly remind you who created and enforced the law and that they operate within it daily. Such protests are not only ignored but could lead to harsher treatment, potentially worsening one's situation. At that moment, in that place, I became a detainee in the eyes of the police. The law that states one cannot be held beyond 24 hours without a court order seemed meaningless here, especially for someone without political connections or influential status. With a brief word of thanks to the officers who had brought us to the station, Mr. Q shook their hands and left. I felt like a lion trapped in a zoo cage.

CHAPTER FOUR

WAITING FOR MY BODY SEARCH

While standing in line, awaiting my turn for documentation and the search of my pockets and body for any incriminating items–a routine check to prevent detainees from escaping or causing harm to themselves or others–I experienced a level of anxiety unparalleled in my entire life. The policemen who had brought me to the detention centre offered no words of explanation or preparation, leaving my mind in a state of unease about what lay ahead. Never before had I found myself so close to such an inconceivable situation, one that forced me to confront the possibility of suffering consequences for events I neither caused nor could have anticipated. Just 36 hours earlier, I had been laughing and joking with colleagues at our company's social club after work, exchanging playful banter and humorous stories in an atmosphere of camaraderie. Little did I realise that within a day, I would be thrust into what felt like a personal Armageddon–a place where the forces of darkness seemed to overshadow every glimmer of hope.

    I found myself in an agonising predicament, accused of stealing a Volkswagen Beetle. The situation was distressing as I had, albeit indirectly, played a significant role in facilitating the purchase of the car. The funds had been sourced through a contract to which I contributed without seeking feedback or a share–an enigma within the cultural norms of our society. What made the ordeal even more perplexing was that I already owned a Peugeot 504 Saloon, parked in the same compound from which the Beetle was stolen. As I awaited my turn to face the unknown depths of interrogation, my mind was flooded with countless unsettling scenarios. Chief among my concerns was how my neighbours would react upon hearing of my detention. What would they think of me, a long-standing Secretary of the Landlord Association who had held that position since moving to the area eight years ago?

Equally troubling was the thought of my colleagues at work, who had always regarded me with respect and admiration. How would they perceive me after such a scandal? How would the management, my employer, respond when the news of my arrest inevitably reached them? These questions weighed heavily on me, leaving me in a state of profound uncertainty and despair. Within two hours, I found myself in the queue, where I was weighed on a scale. Reflecting on what I had weighed that morning before leaving my bed, I estimated that I must have lost about 3 kilograms. I felt extraordinarily light and hydrated, and as I looked at myself, I could vividly imagine my leanness, brought about by circumstances beyond my control. It was as if a gust of wind could easily blow me off my feet. Health-wise, I was at a crossroads.

My hands were sweating profusely, to the point where I had to wipe them on my trousers every five minutes. By nature, I tend to sweat heavily in hot weather, but the situation worsened under the discomfort of inexplicable stress. I recalled a particularly memorable occasion when I was returning to Nigeria after a month-long holiday in Europe. Upon disembarking at Murtala Muhammed International Airport and completing Immigration procedures, I was approached by a Customs officer during the luggage inspection. Sarcastically, he asked whether I was not carrying drugs, interpreting my appearance as a sign of guilt or fear of breaking narcotics laws. I calmly assured him that I was willing to undergo any screening necessary to prove my innocence. As he inspected my belongings, he came across my office identity card in a small bag I had taken from my hand luggage. At that moment, his demeanour shifted. Offering an unreserved apology, he allowed the matter to drop immediately, and we parted with a firm handshake.

The only idea that came to mind–a seemingly foolish one–was to wonder what might happen if I refused to be taken to the cell, asserting my innocence and invoking my rights. In civilised countries where international laws are respected, implemented, and applied to suspects in criminal cases, such as the United States and the United Kingdom, the process is notably different. If arrested on suspicion of an offence, you would be taken to a police station, questioned, and your responses recorded in a written statement. You would then be asked to sign the statement, as it could later be used as evidence if the Crown Prosecution Service decides to pursue prosecution in a court of law. Importantly, you would not be held in police custody for more than 24 hours after the initial arrest unless the case was particularly severe or your release was deemed to pose a serious risk to public safety. In such instances, the police are required to seek and obtain a special licence from the Magistrates' Court to extend the period of detention. While these principles are clear and rigorously upheld in theory, their practical application in certain countries often reveals glaring inconsistencies. On paper, similar regulations exist in our own constitution, but in practice, they are largely symbolic–formalities recorded for appearances' sake. They seem to apply only to the privileged few, such as parliamentarians, senators, and bank executives, when arrested by the Economic and Financial Crimes Commission (EFCC) for misappropriation of public funds or embezzlement of customers' savings.

What distinguishes their cases is the staggering scale of their crimes–often involving billions or even trillions of naira–and their elevated political and social status. These factors ensure that their misdemeanours dominate the headlines of national newspapers. Such high-profile cases attract the most expensive Senior Advocates of Nigeria (SANs), who initially offer their services pro bono, confident that once their influential clients are granted bail, they will be handsomely rewarded. Courts, in turn, appear all too willing to grant bail on both reasonable and unreasonable grounds. This glaring disparity in the application of the law between different groups of citizens has prompted many to ask pointed and bitter questions: 'Are we truly equal under the same laws in the same country?'

Being held in police custody was far worse than confinement in a military guardroom, where soldiers under investigation were separated from their regiment for breaching military regulations. In guardrooms, basic facilities are provided: clean and hygienic toilets, provisions for washing clothes, maintaining personal hygiene, and spaces to rest. Even if a soldier has already been found guilty of an alleged crime, they are not deprived of food or water. In contrast, police custody offers none of these. The detainees are subjected to inhumane conditions, with only two possible postures imposed by the circumstances. The first is sitting, and detainees are not allowed to stand unless ordered to do so by the *president* of the cell–a title given to a fellow detainee designated as the enforcer. The personal choice regarding posture is non-existent; bodyguards enforce compliance, often resorting to intimidation or violence. Signs of reluctance or resistance are met with loud rebukes, quickly followed by harsh, demeaning slaps on both cheeks.

I once witnessed a particularly distressing incident where a man, emaciated to the point of frailty, was forcibly pulled to his feet by bodyguards whose hands, wide and heavy, encircled his waist. It was a pitiful sight. Yet, the police officers on duty paid no attention to the cries and commotion from the cell, intervening only when a detainee exhibited signs of severe mental distress or aggression. On such occasions, they would storm in armed with truncheons and administer brutal beatings, punishing the individual for *disrupting* the order they had established. This *order* was rigidly enforced, with the cell president wielding authority granted by the police. The announcement of his *staff of office* was a public declaration meant to instil fear and compliance among the inmates. The only other permissible posture for detainees was to sit on the bare, concrete floor. The overcrowded cell resembled a cattle truck packed with inmates so tightly that stretching one's legs or lying down was impossible. Each person was forced to fold their legs under them, remaining in this cramped position for as long as their body could endure. The cell was small, poorly ventilated, and grossly inadequate for its population, making the experience unbearable.

From the description provided earlier, I encourage you to imagine the oppressive heat inside an overcrowded, poorly ventilated cell, endured 24/7. Most of the older inmates, having lost their shirts and vests–if they had any upon their incarceration–were left exposed to the relentless combination of heat, sweat, and filth. For those who still wore their vests, originally white at the time of purchase, the absence of washing over an extended period had rendered them brown or even black with grime. None of the inmates had bathed since their confinement began. Interestingly, a special arrangement was made for the president of the group, allowing him to shave, clean himself, and change into a fresh white outfit provided by the police every Friday following the announcement of the selection, referred to as an election. Does it not become a political farce when one is reminded, 'Are you all equal before the law and the constitution of the country?'

CHAPTER FIVE

WELCOME PARTY AT THE CELL

Within three hours at the police station, I was treated like a hardened criminal under military regulations, as though I were about to face a tribunal where my alleged offence would be read out and judged. The same group of policemen still flanked me–one on my right and the other on my left–ready to hand me over to the reception area where I would be locked away, supposedly to prevent me from posing a danger to society. I had already been labelled a car thief despite the lack of any evidence to justify such humiliation. At the detention block, the police receptionist was slow and unwelcoming, while the language used by the three constables at the duty desk was deplorable. They spoke barbarically as if they were old pharaohs, with a tone of authority over everyone in their presence. I observed this in their treatment of three other suspects who were being processed before me. These suspects were from different incidents and brought in by various groups of officers, yet all were subjected to the same degrading treatment. The insults, yelling, and shouting of the constables were better left unquoted and unprinted for any civilised reader.

By the time it was my turn, the process was relatively swift and somewhat less harsh than what I had seen others endure. The officers handed their colleagues a paper on which, presumably, my name, age, and address had been noted. After scribbling something on it, they returned it to the officers, who signed it. I assumed this document contained my detention number.

I was instructed to empty my trouser pockets and turn them inside out for everyone to see they were empty. I was then told to remove my belt and shoes, which were taken away, leaving me barefoot. The officers conducted a body search, patting me down to ensure I was not carrying anything harmful, anything that could cause a disturbance, or anything I could use to escape detention. During the search, one of the policemen made an infuriating remark, clearly aiming to amuse his colleagues. Provoked, I responded sharply, saying, 'Would you like to say that to your father at home?' My retort silenced the room instantly, and no one made another derogatory comment towards me after that. I could not see what happened to the other detainees lined up behind me for the same screening. However, I noticed the policeman who had made the remark left his post and disappeared into the cells for about ten minutes before returning to his position. When he came back, he gave a subtle wink to one of his colleagues. Although I could not decipher his intentions at the time, I sensed a plot was unfolding, which became clearer minutes later. The policeman to whom I made the remark was the last person standing by the door to the cell. On the three previous occasions I had observed, he was the officer stationed at the far end of the screening table and the one who escorted suspects to the cell door. When it was my turn to be taken to the cell, however, he delegated the task to one of the other two officers.

I had no prior experience of police detention, let alone any understanding of how such places were organised or the extent of the policemen's influence over the inmates. As I approached the cell, the first thing I noticed was a man standing at the entrance, dressed entirely in white–a white shirt paired with white knickers. As I attempted to avoid physical contact with him, he seemed to deliberately brush his shoulder or body against mine. Despite my best efforts to squeeze through the narrow space by hugging the doorframe, he persisted in invading my personal space, his actions both deliberate and unsettling. Once inside, I instinctively turned back to look at him, curious about his unusual attire in contrast to the others, who wore their ordinary clothes. As I tried to take in the scene and comprehend the situation, I was suddenly struck by a sharp and devastating slap across my face. Shocked, I turned to see that the policeman who had escorted me to the cell was standing at the door. To my horror, he burst into laughter, clapping his hands in apparent approval of the humiliation I had just endured.

The slap had been delivered by a very tall and imposing young man, approximately 22 years old, who stood behind the man in white. The latter, moments earlier, had violated my boundaries by deliberately brushing against me. As the cell erupted in laughter, it became clear that I had no recourse. The policemen–those ostensibly responsible for the welfare of inmates–had not only condoned the act but had actively enjoyed my humiliation. Their inaction and visible amusement left no doubt that the assault had their tacit approval. By the expressions on the faces of the other inmates, it was apparent that such incidents were neither unusual nor cause for comment. No one protested on my behalf or expressed surprise. Resigned to the reality of my situation, I accepted this as my introduction to the dehumanising experience of being in police custody, a grim lesson in the misuse of authority by government officials.

My second experience of humiliation was even worse than the first. As the sun set and darkness began to envelop the night, the same young man who had slapped me earlier approached me again. This time, he informed me that I would serve as the *Toshiba fan* for the chairman of the cell throughout the night. At first, I did not understand what he meant. It became painfully clear, however, as the hours of my second ordeal began to unfold. To be a *Toshiba fan* for the chairman meant I had to remove my shirt, stand very close to him, and use my shirt to fan him. The chairman would lie on his back or side in one of the corners of the cell, a space he occupied alone. Meanwhile, the rest of us, a crowd of detainees, were crammed together like sardines, sitting on the bare concrete floor with our legs folded tightly to our bodies. There was no space to stretch out, let alone lie down. The rules of the cell, as dictated by the police, or perhaps by the personal whims of the officers on duty, required that all detainees being held on behalf of the Federal Government remain seated, legs folded, for the entirety of their detention. This regulation offered no concessions, no alternatives. While the chairman of the cell enjoyed his privileged position, alongside his self-appointed aide-de-camp (ADC), the rest of us endured the harsh reality of confinement in cramped, dehumanising conditions.

Before delving into details about the cell's current *president* during my detention, it is important to provide a vivid description of the cell itself: its dimensions, the number of detainees, the feeding arrangements, the type and quantity of food provided, and the general conditions within. The cell was a small hall, approximately 12 feet by 15 feet, originally painted light blue but now reduced to a dingy dark brown. The discolouration was caused by years of neglect, compounded by the constant rubbing of sweaty bodies and hands against the walls. The floor, made of plain concrete, had no covering and appeared to have been laid some thirty years before my arrival. Over time, much of the cement surface had chipped away through continuous wear and tear. The ceiling, which was presumably painted white when new, had taken on a grimy, multi-coloured appearance due to years of accumulated moisture from inmates' breath. With no ventilation to disperse the carbon dioxide that hung heavily in the air, the environment was suffocating.

No decent society would keep its pets–cats or dogs–in such a filthy space if those animals were intended to share their homes. Such conditions might be deemed acceptable only in a setting reminiscent of *Animal Farm*. The stench within the cell was reminiscent of the odour that pervaded the streets when Lagos State contracted the removal of human waste by trucks stationed at roadside locations. Moving away from the state of the floor and walls, let me describe the ventilation. A single small window, permanently fixed with glass, was set high near the roof, beyond the reach of even the tallest detainee. Climbing atop one another to reach it was strictly forbidden and considered a breach of custody regulations, punishable by an extension of the detention period. Judging by its filthy, almost opaque condition, the window seemed never to have been opened since its installation. It was impossible to discern the weather outside through the grime-encrusted glass. The placement and design of the window were intended to prevent escape attempts, but the consequence was a stifling environment, with the window locked shut for the entirety of my captivity.

The most horrific aspect of this situation was the oppressive heat generated by the overcrowding. With 49 people crammed into this tiny cell, the conditions were unbearable. Even without wearing a shirt, sweat would pour from your body, leaving you feeling as though you were being roasted alive. These were the harsh realities of life in police detention. It would be incomplete to discuss detention without mentioning the general appearance of the detainees. Broadly speaking, there are two distinct classes of individuals within the detention camp. The first class comprises those who maintain special relationships with the police, while the second class consists of those who have no one to inquire after them or provide the necessary inducements–referred to in Nigerian parlance as *shaking the hands of the policemen*. These inducements often translate into royal treatment for the privileged detainees.

The physical conditions of these two groups are starkly contrasting and difficult to articulate fully. Those in the first class have external connections–relatives or acquaintances–who ensure their well-being by offering tokens or bribes to the police. This external support ensures they receive preferential treatment. They are relatively well-fed and allowed out of the cells into the corridors, where they can enjoy fresh air–a luxury denied to the second class. In contrast, the second class, devoid of such connections, are emaciated to the point where they resemble walking skeletons or mummified remains. Their bodies are reduced to little more than bones, their stomachs sunken as if emptied by surgical removal. When they stand, one can practically feel their backbones from their stomachs; their torsos are as flat as a parched pond.

Another distinguishing factor is the overwhelming odour within the cells. Basic hygiene is non-existent–no toothbrushes for cleaning teeth, no shaving sticks for grooming, and no provisions for bathing or even washing one's face with clean water. The stench is pervasive, a grim testament to the dehumanising conditions. In truth, one might question whether even the German regime under Adolf Hitler subjected Jews to worse conditions in detention camps during the Second World War. The plight of these detainees could be likened to living genocide. Those in the second class are merely surviving, their lives drained of vitality, reduced to hollow shells of existence. The police have all but taken their lives, leaving them breathing only for the sake of biological continuity, as though their journey to their final destination–be it a metaphorical bus stop or the airport of their maker–has yet to conclude.

On the day of my release, when I was finally told I could return home, I stepped outside the detention building and felt the fresh air–air I had been deprived of for almost three weeks. As I took my first steps out, something caught my attention to my left. Turning my head, I saw six people lined up in front of the entrance to the building. Their appearance stopped me in my tracks, and I wept. They were emaciated, resembling dried stockfish, and were so filthy that I was certain their families–wives, children, or other relations–would not recognise them without reintroductions. Even then, their loved ones might either break down in tears or recoil in fear, mistaking them for mentally ill strangers. This was the result of how the police had confined them in the cell without trial or any recourse to the court of law. These individuals were denied the opportunity to either prove their innocence and regain their freedom or, if found guilty, face lawful punishment.

Some of these detainees, I later learned, had been in that wretched state for more than 15 years. It was a barbaric and Napoleonic violation of human dignity. How could such inhumane treatment exist in a country claiming to have a government elected by the people, for the people? Yet this is the very institution we have entrusted to protect and defend us.

CHAPTER SIX

SURVIVAL OF THE FITTEST

Sometimes, circumstances arise that compel one to accept situations they would never have contemplated under normal conditions. As situations change, regularity must often give way to irregularity, adapting to the demands of my circumstances. This, perhaps, is what defines a man. History teaches us that no condition is permanent, and man must, like a chameleon, adjust his outward behaviour to reflect his environment, often as a means of self-preservation. Before I had even glimpsed the interior of the cell, I resolved to follow a course of action, regardless of how long the police might decide to detain me during their investigation. Whether I would be charged and brought to trial, released on bail pending further enquiries, or freed outright for lack of evidence against me, I remained steadfast. I knew I was innocent. I had unshakeable faith in God, with whom I maintained a constant spiritual connection, and I was sure He would not abandon me. My trust in the Lord, whom I served with unwavering devotion, sustained me. With that confidence, I was optimistic that this ordeal would eventually become a significant chapter in the story of my life.

From the outset, I made decisions regarding specific aspects of my predicament. First and foremost, I resolved not to consume any food or drink during my incarceration, no matter how long it lasted. This decision was rooted in my determination to avoid any health issues arising from the consumption of food or water in such unhygienic conditions. Moreover, I wanted to eliminate the need to use the inmates' toilet facilities, which I could only imagine were in a deplorable state. If the cell was in such squalor, what condition might the toilet be in? The thought was beyond comprehension. Prevention, as they say, is better than cure. For twenty-one full days and nights, I neither ate nor drank anything, so I did not visit the toilet. This commitment to my principles became a cornerstone of my sense of decency and hygiene throughout the ordeal.

Secondly, I engaged freely with some of the other inmates, listening to their stories, the allegations against them, and what they knew about others in the cell, particularly those who seemed to receive preferential, almost royal treatment from the policemen on duty. The information I gathered from my fellow detainees can be summarised as follows:

1. The cell President during my time in detention, elevated to a position of privilege by the police, relished the status bestowed upon him. One of the perks of his role was the opportunity to stand out from the other inmates. The police supplied him with white dress weekly, and his meals were of a distinctly higher quality than those provided to the rest of us. Upon critical reflection, the situation seemed to foster an environment where crime was tacitly encouraged

rather than deterred. The correctional measures, ostensibly designed to reform offenders, fell far short of public expectations. Instead of serving as a deterrent or a source of moral instruction, detention in Nigeria during my experience lacked any reformative impact and failed to discourage criminal behaviour. Alarmingly, hardened criminals were elevated in status and afforded privileges by the same system funded by the public purse–an establishment ostensibly created to protect society from such individuals. This misplaced glorification only served to embolden them, enabling them to inflict harsher harm upon their eventual return to society. Even innocent suspects caught in the web of detention might view these criminals as figures of admiration and role models to emulate, further perpetuating the cycle of crime.

2. Little information was known about the bodyguard. He was arrested for forcing himself on an underage girl in the school where he was serving as a security guard, and was also known as a chieftain of a gang member along mile 2 to Badagry road. He often boasted about the business tycoons whose smuggled goods he had successfully escorted from Cotonou in the Republic of Benin to Badagry. With unabashed arrogance, he claimed that no government official–whether police or customs–had ever managed to disrupt his operations. His tales grew darker as he bragged about the number of government agents he had eliminated in the course of his duties, his words laced with an unsettling pride. Known by numerous nicknames, he resided in a shanty hut along the route to Badagry. This location, he explained, was strategic; if trouble arose, he could dive into the lagoon and swim

across the border to safety. His lifestyle during his so-called *hay days* was one of excess and indulgence. He claimed to have rarely drunk water, instead subsisting on illicit gin and Indian hemp, both of which were as readily available to him as sachet water at roadside stalls or bus garages. His voice was deep, gravelly, and cracked–a telltale sign of years of marijuana use, which he openly admitted was a daily habit. My only direct encounter with him was when he greeted me upon my arrival in the cell with a slap, a crude initiation ritual. He then forced me to serve as a *Toshiba fan* for the cell President–a humiliating induction into the detention system. Beyond that unpleasant interaction, we never exchanged another word.

After spending two days in the cell, I could discern a sense of remorse in the bodyguard's behaviour. However, given the lifestyle he was accustomed to, offering apologies, whether for intentional or unintentional wrongdoings, appeared to be absent from his doctrine or dictionary of life. I was informed that he suspected me because of the way I interacted with the other detainees, believing I might be an undercover agent sent to extract information. He never once looked in my direction, and I felt no need to look in his; we became like two sides of a coin or parallel lines that would never meet.

Among the detainees, there were around ten individuals whose lives had been utterly devastated by the prolonged period of their separation from society. They were emaciated, their physical frames as fragile as broomsticks–men we might once have described as *ten pence bones and two pence flesh*. Some of them, in all earnestness, could no longer recall how many years they had spent in police custody. There were no clocks on the walls, and none of the inmates owned a wristwatch to keep track of time or date. Although, I am not asserting whether the reasons given for their arrests were valid or not–the police alone held the records of their alleged crimes under the guise of *ongoing investigations*–I could not help but feel deeply ashamed as a human being. Whatever offences they might have committed–be it robbery, murder, or rape–they should have been arraigned for trial. If found guilty by a court of law, they ought to have been sentenced and sent to proper prisons.

Regardless of the crime a citizen commits, they deserve to be brought before the appropriate criminal court, with their offence graded according to its severity. Allowing individuals to languish in such deplorable conditions–reduced to what can only be described as human *boiled vegetables*–is a profound disservice to justice and human dignity. Being held in a custody cell that lacks basic human necessities, such as drinking water, facilities for washing one's face or body, or even adequate space to stretch one's legs, amounts to a violation of human rights. In such places, detainees are denied even the bare minimum, such as a clean floor or a simple mat to lie on. The police have effectively created conditions for suspects that are worse than those in animal zoos. Many detainees become so filthy and malnourished that they are barely recognisable, their bodies emaciated to the extent that only their heads seem to remain. Their faces grow gaunt and elongated, and it is no exaggeration to suggest that, without prior warning, their wives, children, or close relations might pass by them in the street without recognising them.

One of the non-governmental organisations (NGOs) must be empowered to conduct routine inspections of police detention facilities across the federation. These NGOs should be allowed to document their findings on the appalling conditions of these cells and submit detailed reports with recommendations to the Ministry of Internal Affairs. Such investigations would serve as a lens into the reality of these cells, revealing conditions so horrifying that they would shock Nigerians. Furthermore, the Federal Government, as the employer of the police and the authority responsible for overseeing detention facilities, could find itself summoned before the International Court of Justice in The Hague to explain how it justifies such treatment of its citizens.

Detention facilities are ostensibly intended to maintain peace and order in communities by removing disruptive elements. However, in practice, they often devolve into centres of power struggles among inmates. Individuals who exhibit the most thuggish behaviour–those who smoke Indian hemp and display readiness to engage in violent acts–frequently rise to positions of influence within the cell. For instance, the role of *president* within the detention hierarchy is rumoured not to be based on good behaviour or neutrality but on what benefits the individual can provide to the police. These so-called *elections* are reportedly held every Friday, underscoring the pervasive corruption and manipulation within the system. Such accounts highlight the urgent need for reform in Nigeria's detention facilities, not only to restore dignity to those detained but also to uphold the principles of justice and human rights.

Life in the cell was far from dull, given the variety of individuals confined within its walls. Some inmates enjoyed special relationships with the police officers on duty, creating a noticeable divide among prisoners. I recall one such man whose family brought him meals three times daily. When I say meals, I mean proper, well-prepared, and varied dishes. In the morning, his family would deliver freshly baked bread, known as *singer* in those days–now referred to as Ghana bread–accompanied by sardines and fried eggs. By afternoon, it might be rice with vegetables or pepper soup. The evening brought yet another type of meal. The most striking aspect of this arrangement was the officers' deference to this class of inmate. It was almost surreal to witness the honour they extended to such individuals, considering their criminal records. In this particular man's case, he was implicated in the embezzlement of significant sums through bank robbery–a crime that, one would assume, should garner no special treatment.

In stark contrast, the rest of us endured a harsh and demeaning routine. Meals, if they could be called that, were served in shared, battered plastic containers. Breakfast arrived around 9:30 a.m., consisting of poorly cooked corn and beans mixed with pepper. Each container came with a single spoon, which had to be passed around. Every inmate was permitted only two scoops before relinquishing the container and spoon to the next person. The health implications of this unsanitary practice were alarming, yet no one in authority seemed to care. Beyond its scant nutritional value, the food's inadequacy reflected the indifference to our well-being. What could three spoonfuls of such a meagre meal do for an adult, let alone sustain someone through a day?

Time, an abstract concept in the cell, was irrelevant. Wristwatches were prohibited, and no clocks adorned the walls.

Without plans, ambitions, or activities to pursue, time became meaningless. Unlike prisons, where structured schedules and dining areas offer some semblance of normalcy, the cell felt like a void–isolated and detached from the outside world. There were no radios, newspapers, or other means to stay informed. We might as well have been sealed in a collapsed underground tunnel, cut off entirely from civilisation. The conditions were oppressive. Overcrowding, coupled with the stifling heat, ensured that most inmates eventually abandoned their shirts or vests. Those who clung to their garments wore filthy, sweat-stained rags, far removed from their original white fabric. Washing facilities were non-existent, and bathing was out of the question. Days, weeks, and even months passed without any opportunity for personal hygiene. Amidst this squalor, special privileges were reserved for the *president* of the cell, who was permitted to shave, clean himself, and change his white attire weekly. Such disparity starkly contradicted the oft-repeated assertion that *all are equal before the law and constitution of this country.* In practice, equality remained an elusive ideal, a mere political slogan devoid of substance.

CHAPTER SEVEN

BEHIND THE SCENE

The Yoruba people, in one of their known proverbs, say: 'The eagle that soars in the air might not be aware that those on the ground are observing its every movement.' Another similar proverb states: 'A corpse lying in the mortuary is oblivious to the frantic efforts of those making burial preparations.' While the second proverb may not directly apply to my situation, it aptly captures the experience of those left to organise the burial – selecting clothes for the deceased, digging the grave, arranging the funeral service in a church or mosque, and securing transportation for the body. The situation becomes even more distressing when foul play or criminal activity is suspected.

In Nigeria, when a motor accident occurs, it is disheartening that instead of other road users stopping to offer assistance, many simply look away and ignore the victim, leaving them to their fate. Countless lives have been lost that could otherwise have been saved. Despite trying to digest Nigeria's road regulations, I have not found any provision explicitly stating that motorists are prohibited from helping accident victims or stranded drivers, whether due to a vehicle breakdown, an armed robbery, or an accident. The predominant deterrent is fear – not of the victim but of law enforcement agents who may complicate matters for the good Samaritan.

As a nation, we have yet to incorporate First Aid and resuscitation procedures into our driving lessons and tests. Thus, in such emergencies, the least we can do is transport the injured to the nearest hospital, whether privately or government-owned. Unfortunately, many hospitals, citing regulations, demand police reports before accepting accident victims for treatment. This requirement has tragically resulted in countless avoidable deaths. Hospitals justify their stance by arguing that the victim might be an armed robber, and they fear repercussions from the police for aiding a suspected criminal. However, from a human rights perspective, even armed robbers are entitled to medical care and should be treated to ensure they can survive and face justice for their crimes.

Another issue is the financial burden of hospital bills, which can run into millions of naira. Often, the victim's family is too impoverished to bear such costs and may hesitate to appear at the hospital altogether. This highlights a systemic problem: hospitals, fearing harassment from law enforcement, sometimes pay substantial sums to extricate themselves from such situations. This reminds me of a particular incident that I found profoundly distressing and utterly unacceptable in a civilised society. It involved my friend, or perhaps more accurately, a social acquaintance, whom I occasionally met whenever we crossed paths in the Government Reservation Area (GRA) of Ikeja. For this account, I shall refer to him as Mr F. He had a bond with his sister, whom he loved and cherished dearly. She was his confidant and closest companion. At the time, she was an undergraduate at the

University of Ibadan (UI). Mr F was very protective of her, often driving to Ibadan in his car to pick her up at the start of university vacations and returning her when classes resumed.

On one such occasion, while driving her back to Ibadan to resume her studies, tragedy struck. For reasons unknown–but certainly not due to speeding, as Mr F was always cautious and never drove beyond 50 mph–the vehicle suddenly veered off the road, swerving from one side to the other, before crashing into the bush. The impact left both passengers severely injured. He suffered a fractured leg, but his sister's injuries were far more critical; she was immobilised but remained conscious enough to respond when spoken to. Drawing on his military training and sheer endurance, he managed to crawl out of the wreckage. Despite his pain, he reached the roadside, removed his shirt, and waved it desperately, trying to signal for help. He gestured urgently, indicating that someone was gravely injured inside the car.

For over two agonising and heart-wrenching hours, vehicles sped past without stopping. Among them were police vehicles and even military-marked cars, yet no one paused to investigate the situation. In desperation, Mr F crawled back to the car to check on his sister's condition. She was still breathing but had lost significant amounts of blood and was unable to speak. Undeterred, he returned to the roadside, pleading with passing motorists, but another hour slipped by before someone finally stopped. It was after 10 p.m. when a Good Samaritan noticed him waving and reversed to his location. The stranger accompanied him back to the wreckage. Tragically, by the time they reached his sister, she had succumbed to her injuries. Mr F was eventually transported to a hospital in Ibadan, carrying the lifeless body of his beloved sister. His leg, swollen grotesquely from the fracture, required urgent medical attention. Yet, despite the ordeal and the indifference he faced, he survived to recount this harrowing experience.

This story serves as a sobering reminder of the apathy that often pervades our society, where even those entrusted with law enforcement or military duties fail to act with compassion. But for the grace of God, he survived to bear witness to this tragic episode–a testament to resilience in the face of unimaginable adversity.

Back to my experience in the cell. I refused to come out whenever my name was called. Despite this, my fellow landlords from the area continued to show up at the Ikeja police station. I stayed hidden because I was too ashamed to be seen in my state. I was dressed in nothing but a vest, which had turned from its original white to a grimy brown, darker even than the cell floor. The unbearable heat, intensified by the carbon dioxide generated from the collective breathing of the inmates, forced me to remove my shirt, and I could no longer trace where it was. My eyes were heavy with sleep deprivation, my legs were swollen from being denied the simple act of stretching, and my joints throbbed with crushing aches. My stomach had flattened against my backbones as I refused to eat or drink. Adding insult to injury, I had withdrawn from the other detainees, only engaging with them when I thought they might share some information. I hoped to learn more about the reasons for their detention or uncover details about life in the cell that might shed light on my predicament.

The police officers on duty occasionally entered the cell with their noses covered, either with a handkerchief or their hands, to mask the stench. On one such occasion, a policeman made a derogatory remark, seemingly intended to amuse himself and his colleagues. He said, 'They say you're a big man and a landlord. So, why haven't your family or friends come to get you out of here? If you refuse to eat the food the government gives us money to buy for detainees, you'll die here. Do you know how many people have died and been buried unceremoniously? What are you asking people in here? This is our territory. Whatever happens here, nobody questions us.' Another officer took it a step further, asking if I was a lawyer or a journalist. He concluded by saying, 'Don't assume you're important just because you're in our custody. If you were truly important, someone would have ensured your freedom by now.'

In earnest, my thoughts were not aligned with theirs, and my aims ran parallel to theirs, leaving no point of intersection or meaningful interaction. It was not my situation that troubled me so deeply, but rather the appalling conditions endured by the other inmates. As I have moderately described, their plight defies adequate description. The length of time many of them had already spent–and were likely to continue spending–in detention was both unimaginable and unjustifiable. The discriminatory treatment deliberately orchestrated by the authorities, under whose supervision they were held, seemed to belong to an entirely different reality. I was convinced that American soldiers captured by the Vietnamese regime during the Vietnam War had been treated more humanely. Despite the Vietnamese government's disregard for United Nations Human Rights Laws, the accounts provided by American prisoners of war (POWs) described treatment far more favourable than what we were enduring in Nigerian police detention.

One midday, I heard my name being called and was summoned to the police reception table. As was my custom, I refused to respond, assuming it was either a visitor or perhaps my wife bringing food, despite my strict instructions for her not to do so. After about thirty minutes, a stranger in civilian clothes appeared at the cell entrance and asked for the person bearing my name. At that moment, I raised my hand, and he informed me that the Divisional Police Officer wished to see me in his office. To my shock, as I prepared to leave, the inmates began bidding me farewell. Some said, 'Goodbye, send our regards to your family,' while others pleaded, 'Tell the world what we are going through here.' Their words nearly broke my heart. Over time, I had become one of them–part of their fraternity–and departing from them felt deeply emotional. Tears flowed freely when one of them implored, 'Remember us in your prayers and share our plight with the Nigerian public.'

I could not control the torrent of emotions that overcame me. When I was handed my shoes, belt, and wristwatch, I ran back to the cell to take a final mental snapshot of its grim reality. Though I had no camera, the haunting image of that place remains etched in my memory and will stay with me for the rest of my life. As I entered the office which I was ushered into, the first people I noticed were two boys. They appeared to be of similar age: one was my first son, and the other was the son of the tenant living on the ground floor of my house. For reasons I could not quite identify, they did not greet me. They were as silent as lifeless figures, their demeanour inscrutable. Within ten minutes, the senior officer arrived. After introducing himself, he instructed the detective who had brought me to the office to produce the papers authorising my discharge from detention.

The officers confirmed they had found no clues to lead them to the stolen car. At that point, the Divisional Police Officer declared, 'In the meantime, we shall allow you to return home and resume your duties. Should there be any need for further clarification, we will invite you back to the station for additional questioning.' I was dumbfounded. For three weeks, I was detained, yet no evidence had emerged against me. Why, I wondered, can't the Nigerian police adopt modern investigative practices, as seen in civilised countries? In more advanced societies, when an individual is arrested for a crime or suspected involvement in one, they are taken to the station where a statement is recorded and read back to them for confirmation before being signed. Within 24 hours, the suspect–at this stage legally recognised as such–must either be released or, if there is sufficient suspicion linking them to the crime, the police must seek a court order from a magistrate to extend their detention. Failing this, the suspect is either released on self-recognition or granted bail with a guarantor.

In cases where evidence is insufficient–whether due to lack of physical proof or eyewitness accounts–the police must obtain a court order to retain custody of the individual. For serious crimes such as murder, rape, or grievous bodily harm, suspects are remanded in prison detention while their case file is transferred to the Criminal Investigation Department (CID) to determine whether enough evidence exists to prosecute the matter in court. I recalled a friend of mine who, during conversations about the failures of politicians and government institutions, would always respond, 'We are getting there.' He believed the country was making progress, but I often struggled to understand his stance. Questions of *how?* and *when?* never seemed to trouble him. According to him, even if those in charge were neither working towards improvement nor praying for it, the situation would somehow resolve itself. Their sole interest, it seemed, lay in personal gain or superficial contributions to the public interest. For this social malaise, we have a phrase: *I Before Others.*

The matter for which I was detained as a suspect did not end with me being the sole individual implicated. Upon my release, I learned that my first son, who was just 16 years old at the time of the incident, had also been detained in connection with the case. I was unaware of this while in custody, as he was held in a separate cell within the same Ikeja Police Station. Furthermore, my tenant, who occupied the ground floor apartment of my house, and her son–of the same age as mine–were also detained.

I was informed that the owner of the missing car, in a display of uncontrollable exuberance during a gathering of his family and friends, boasted that he would spare no effort in uncovering the truth behind the case. He claimed he was prepared to have my entire compound locked down if that was what it would take to resolve the matter. The car owner reportedly told the police–or was perhaps advised by family members to allege–that my tenant might be culpable. This tenant, however, was a woman of impeccable character–a gentlelady, a former London resident, a fashion designer with both national and international acclaim, and a member of the same church I attended in Ogba. She was also well-connected in the media industry. Once news of her arrest spread, her associates and connections rallied to secure her release from the clutches of the police.

The fact that the Nigerian police could detain a minor is a troubling issue that I will not delve into extensively in this book. In

Nigeria, it is not uncommon for instructions to come from above, for influence to play a role, or for money to exchange hands. My son, unfortunately, became a victim simply because he was my son. Mr Q, influenced by interested parties around him, reported to the police that my son might be involved in the disappearance of the car from my premises. This boy was nothing more than a typical schoolboy with all the attributes of youthful behaviour. He had never been violent, and no one could claim to have seen him causing trouble or associating with wayward or irresponsible peers.

Their goal was clear: to tarnish my name irreparably. When people are determined to destroy another, they aim for the head, seeking total annihilation. They cut the tree at its roots, knowing that cutting the stem alone allows the possibility of regrowth. However, they forget the profound truth that there is no situation God cannot change. My son and the tenant's son were released on the same day as I was, though they attended a separate briefing from mine and at a different time. From the analysis of the chain of events, I was convinced beyond reasonable doubt that, were it not for the young age of my daughters, Mr Q might have been compelled to ask the police to arrest my wife. There seemed to be no limit to the desperation some individuals would embrace, as the malevolence within them often overpowered their sense of judgement. Such people appeared unable to discern the boundary between right and wrong. Their sole ambition seemed to be destruction–ruthless and unrelenting–until no trace or foundation of the victim remained, as though the person had never existed or borne their name.

The instruction I gave to my secretary–to inform my friends and associates that I was unwell and receiving treatment in an undisclosed hospital, rather than revealing I was in police custody–did not remain tenable for long. The reality was that I could not procure an official medical certificate to corroborate such a claim. Moreover, my friends were well aware that I took my work seriously and that my absence from the club after office hours was highly unusual. The club was our informal gathering place, where we exchanged anecdotes–work-related and personal–on a daily basis. By a twist of fate, or perhaps by divine design, a member of the Nigeria Airways cabin crew resided not far from my house. Similarly, another lady, employed in the airline's Accounts department, lived with her family within shouting distance of my residence. Although we had exchanged visits occasionally in the past, it was only a matter of days before my absence became the subject of speculation within the neighbourhood. The news of my disappearance began to spread across the company premises like the discovery of an unexploded Second World War bomb unearthed in my backyard.

CHAPTER EIGHT

POLICING AND PROSECUTION IN NIGERIA

Permit me to take you back to my root once more–I am Yoruba. The Yoruba people, in one of their proverbial sayings, state, 'The eagle that soars in the sky does not realise that those on the ground are closely watching its flight.' This means that whatever one does in private, no matter how shrouded in darkness, secrecy, or confidentiality, will eventually come to light. When that happens, particularly if the individual is held in high regard, it can lead to profound disappointment.

In the world of national newspapers, sensational headlines on the front pages are key to attracting buyers. To remain competitive in the fast-paced newspaper industry, a publisher must not only stay ahead by securing the latest news but also present it in a way that sparks readers' eagerness to grab a copy as soon as it hits the stands. Achieving this requires cultivating connections with influential figures who can provide advanced insights into significant developments in government or business. It was common for sensational news to delve into unfounded rumours, yet such incidents rarely led to a loss of public patronage or legal action for defamation. To avoid such repercussions, it was often sufficient to offer an unreserved apology, admitting that the source of information was neither accurate nor authentic. This practice was widely accepted as standard and aligned with the principles of international public trust. However, errors were frequently handled differently within government establishments. Rather than acknowledging mistakes, authorities often sought to conceal them, employing administrative tools or cloaking the issue in jargon, such as deeming it with terms like *private, confidential,* and *secrecy.* These terms were commonly used to shield themselves from the scrutiny of public critics.

For instance, if a bystander were arrested or subjected to inhumane treatment–beaten to the point of unconsciousness or even death–a concerned observer might question the police or military personnel involved. Such inquiries, based on moral or religious grounds (since many people claim to follow one faith or another), would demand accountability. Those responsible should explain their actions clearly, citing the specific laws, rules, or regulations that justified their conduct. This level of transparency is both a moral obligation and fundamental expectation in a just society.

The Nigeria Police Force (NPF), in many instances, has acted as though it is not taxpayer money funding their recruitment, training, uniforms, accommodation, salaries, and allowances, including annual holidays. At times, their conduct resembles that of an invading force from another world, descending to destroy the enemy's camp. The notion that they are Nigerians, trained, equipped, and paid to protect the very people they serve, seems unfathomable. Merely because someone comes to a police station to report an incident does not automatically imply that the individual being reported is guilty of the alleged offence. In law, it is accepted that a person is a suspect, not guilty until a thorough investigation has been conducted and sufficient evidence is established. Before the investigation begins, the law provides for the person to be granted bail, provided they can meet the established bail conditions and present a suitable surety. All that is required at this stage is for a statement to be taken and signed to verify the authenticity of what the suspect has said.

At this point, the individual remains a suspect and is not deemed guilty of any offence until the allegations are proven beyond reasonable doubt and a judge in a court of law is satisfied with the evidence. In some cases, the suspect's passport may be seized as a precautionary measure, ensuring their availability for the scheduled court hearing. Once the investigation is completed, the case file should be sent to the legal department. In developed countries, this independent body is known as the Crime Prosecution Service (CPS), whose responsibility is to assess whether the evidence gathered is substantial enough to warrant public funds for prosecution.

In Nigeria, the Attorney General of the Federation (AGF), a political appointee of the President within the government cabinet, has often been reported to overrule the recommendations of the Public Prosecution Service, either in the interest of the ruling political party or, as was alleged during President Muhammadu Buhari's regime, due to personal gain. As claimed, case files were seized and locked away, never returned to the Public Prosecution Office, driven by the AGF's vested interests. The Economic and Financial Crimes Commission (EFCC) accused the AGF of blocking many money laundering cases. This is a frequent point of contention for opposition parties, who have raised concerns of political victimisation whenever their members were charged with campaign irregularities.

Contrary to the dictates of the law, I was wrongfully charged with an offence I did not commit, and the police department handled the case in a manner that was neither lawful nor humane. Their actions were marked by callousness and a blatant disregard for my fundamental rights, resulting in my detention for three weeks without any respect for due process. This experience underscores the critical need for the government to take decisive action to safeguard the rule of law and ensure the protection of citizens' rights. Without such measures, the judicial system cannot function as it should.

Reflecting on the Buhari/Idiagbon administration's War Against Indiscipline in 1984, one recalls that, despite instances of personnel abusing their authority to perpetrate acts of cruelty, the government made a concerted effort to uphold the law. The result was a nation where citizens adhered to rules and regulations. Today, however, faith in the judicial system–particularly in the Nigeria Police Force–has significantly eroded. This loss of trust stems from their persistent failure to respect the Constitution and their role as enforcers of justice. Without a renewed commitment to accountability and reform, the justice system will remain a source of disillusionment for the very people it is meant to serve.

CHAPTER NINE

THE SELECTION OF PRESIDENT FOR THE DETAINEES

As I have briefly discussed the nature of governance in the cell earlier in some pages of this book, let me go into more detail about the process of appointing the president. Democracy appears to have no place in the regulations or practices of Nigerian police officers when it comes to detainees. Within the confines of our cell, the election of a *President* was a weekly ritual. It was routinely announced around 10:00 a.m. every Friday by one of the duty officers at the reception desk. The process was executed with robotic precision, devoid of warmth or humour among the inmates. The police officers, however, seemed to relish their role, acting as though they were the chairmen of the Independent National Electoral Commission (INEC). I observed no nomination papers, campaigns, or competition among the inmates. No one approached others with promises to address the chaos in the cell, improve the meagre, unpalatable meals, or enhance the general welfare of the detainees. At precisely 10:00 a.m., after the so-called breakfast–which, in terms of taste, smell, and portion, I would not even offer to a dog–one of the duty officers would stand at the entrance to the cell and announce:

> 'Attention, everybody. I bring you good news this morning. After due consideration and consultation, Mr [dash] has been unanimously elected as your president for this week. We expect you to cooperate with him. Thank you.'

Throughout my time in the cell, the same man was consistently chosen as *President*. There was nothing remotely electoral about the process or its procedures.

WHO WAS THE APPOINTED PRESIDENT OF THE DETENTION?

According to the information gathered, he had booked accommodation at a hotel in Agege for several nights. During his absence, while a cleaner was tidying his room, she accidentally discovered guns and a cache of ammunition hidden under his bed. At the time of the discovery, he was away from the hotel, enjoying himself. The hotel manager promptly alerted the police to investigate the matter. When he returned late that night, heavily intoxicated, he was confronted by the police and arrested on suspicion of possessing dangerous items that could be used to harm or kill innocent people. He was taken to Ikeja Police Station, where the records revealed he was a figure of some notoriety due to his lineage and the reputation of his family. In trades, expertise is essential, and his notoriety earned him the title of *president of the cell*–a position he held for life, or at least for as long as he remained in custody. Perhaps someone higher in the criminal hierarchy might one day replace him, but that had yet to occur. Questions lingered about his identity and his family background.

Those familiar with history and the media might recall the sensational case involving criminals who specialised in robbing Peugeot 404 cars at gunpoint some years ago. The most infamous among them was Oyenusi. A Divisional Police Officer, who acted as their godfather and shielded them from the law, was also implicated in these crimes. His name was George Iyamu. After thorough investigations and comprehensive legal proceedings, he was publicly executed alongside other members of the gang. The *president* of the cell in which I was detained happened to be the son of the police officer involved in that trial. He, undoubtedly, inherited the *trade* from his father. His rise to power within police custody required no thorough investigation. In Nigerian terms, boldness, coupled with the ability to spread money through every corner of society, often propels individuals to limitless heights. In such circumstances, even the sky may not suffice as a boundary.

This brings us to another, more recent case involving a prominent politician and a retired senior military officer who were jailed for money laundering. Newspapers reported that the politician's wife was permitted to bring him his preferred meals, drinks and immaculately ironed traditional outfits daily in prison. Such a situation epitomises the Nigerian saying, *Man pass man*. In Nigeria, there is little that could occur that would elicit the reaction, *That's impossible.* As the late Jubril Martin Kuye reminded his students in 1959, 'The word *impossible* exists only in the dictionary of fools.'

My sympathy and concern lie with the ordinary people, those without godfathers or the financial means to navigate a corrupt system, who often fall victim to the very individuals employed to protect their lives and property. Frequently, innocent people are arrested for crimes they did not commit, and we can only hope never to find ourselves in such a situation.

At a police station in Nigeria, some basic items are not freely provided. To write a report or statement, one must pay for the paper and pen. After use, the pen must be returned to the officer who lent it, as it is not yours to keep. The number of people who use the same pen in a single day is better imagined than described. Indeed, nothing at a Nigerian police station is free. Without someone influential to intervene on your behalf, you risk being unceremoniously thrown into a cell. It is easy to get into the Nigerian cell, but to get released is a near-impossible ordeal. Police investigations in such cases are notoriously indefinite. They may have a beginning, but unfortunately, they rarely have an end unless a powerful and expensive lawyer steps in to advocate for you. The cost of such legal assistance is often beyond the reach of the average person. Even while going about your legitimate daily activities, you could suddenly find yourself stopped on the street, pushed into a police van, and whisked away without explanation. If you lack the money to extricate yourself from this trap, the police may never inform you of the charges against you. You could be detained indefinitely, possibly until you draw your last breath.

In 1984, during the military regime of Generals Buhari and Idiagbon, I had a profoundly distressing encounter with the Nigerian Police Force. It was an era when many Nigerians at home and abroad, believed the nation was awakening to civilisation and self-respect. The government had introduced the *War Against Indiscipline* (WAI), a programme widely touted as transformative, and it was embraced by some sections of the population with great enthusiasm. However, in a system like Nigeria's, the implementation of such initiatives often deviated from their noble intentions, sometimes spiralling into outright oppression. The Nigerian Police, as the primary enforcers of the policy, bore significant responsibility for its perceived successes or failures. Their mandate to oversee public compliance often gave them unchecked authority. Unfortunately, this power was frequently abused. It is a troubling reality that, when entrusted with even a small measure of authority, some Nigerians in positions of power will overreach, expanding their influence far beyond their original scope. In this instance, the police became tyrannical, mistreating and humiliating ordinary citizens in ways that defied basic humanity. Their actions were not only oppressive but also utterly dehumanising, surpassing anything one might imagine under the control of a supposed adversary like the devil himself.

On one fateful Tuesday, while leaving my workplace, I decided to visit a public market called Aswani. It was an open market that operated exclusively on Tuesdays, and though I had often heard of it, I had never had the opportunity to see it for myself. As I approached the entrance, I was confronted with a horrifying scene. Four hefty policemen were mercilessly beating an elderly woman who appeared old enough to be their mother. To me, such behaviour was unthinkable in a society that claimed to uphold civilisation and the rule of law. Never before had I witnessed such a barbaric act from individuals tasked with enforcing justice. The helpless old woman was at their mercy, and yet, no one dared to intervene or even approach the scene to appeal for compassion on her behalf. The onlookers stood silently, their hands folded, shaking their heads in a collective gesture of sympathy and resignation.

I found the entire situation appalling and inhumane. It reminded me of George Orwell's *Animal Farm*, where the notion of equality is subverted by those who manipulate their strength or authority to dominate others. The offence that provoked this cruel display? The poor woman had been carrying plantains and bananas on her head, likely trying to earn a modest income to feed herself and her family. Her meagre goods, worth no more than ₦150, lay scattered on the ground, the plastic container that had held them smashed to pieces.

Overcome with emotion, I could not hold back my tears. The sight of her broken dignity and desperate condition struck me deeply. It was a vivid and painful reminder of the injustices that ordinary citizens endured under a system designed to protect them but which, instead, exploited and demeaned them. With a spirit of kindness and a determination to intervene, I approached the policemen, pleading with them to release the old woman. I urged them to let her go and nurse the injuries she had sustained, which were visibly severe, covering her face and body. My tone was as polite as I could muster, though internally, I was boiling with rage. How could agents of law enforcement in Nigeria behave so maliciously, so wickedly, and so inhumanely towards a fellow citizen? The public humiliation inflicted by uniformed officers on a defenceless woman was both disgraceful and appalling.

At first, they pretended not to see or hear me, perhaps expecting me to walk away. When I persisted in my plea, however, they shifted their attention to me. What followed was not a dialogue but an escalation of barbaric violence. I was beaten, mercilessly, as though I were a stepchild–treated with the kind of cruelty often described in tales of domestic mistreatment, where a new wife sees the child of a previous marriage as an obstacle to her full affection from the husband. Much like those stories, I was punished harshly for daring to speak out, with no regard for fairness or humanity.

What struck me most was the sheer inhumanity of the act. Even an illegal immigrant discovered hiding in a foreign country would not have been treated with such disdain and brutality. I naively thought this beating would be the end of my ordeal, but I was wrong–it was merely the beginning of a harrowing journey at the hands of those meant to serve and protect.

The gathered crowd, drawn by the commotion, watched in silent horror as I was thrown into the back of a police van. The vehicle, already loaded with refuse seized during their patrol, was now my prison. The stench was unbearable, a nauseating mix of rotting fruit, broken eggs, and other decomposing food items. The force with which they shoved me inside caused my clothes to become enmeshed in filth, and I sustained a bruised leg in the process–a wound I had no time to examine, let alone complain about. The van then began a chaotic journey through the suburbs of Lagos. From one street to another, it bumped, swerved, and braked abruptly, deliberately tossing me around inside. It was evident that the rough handling of the vehicle was intentional, as I could hear the officers in the front seats laughing, glancing back to observe my suffering. Their amusement at my discomfort was a stark reminder of how far removed they were from any sense of duty or decency.

We circled the streets surrounding the market, proceeded to Oshodi, and then moved through the maze of roads leading to Agege Motor Road. Eventually, the truck came to a halt in front of a house. I could only speculate that it belonged to one of the officers. A casually dressed woman emerged, followed by two middle-aged men, and I watched as they unloaded electronic gadgets from the truck's second compartment into the house. The process took nearly 30 minutes, during which it became increasingly clear that these items, likely confiscated from traders, were being converted to private use. After this interlude, the journey resumed at a slower pace. We meandered through the streets of Agege, eventually emerging in Ogba, an area I recognised well. Gradually, we approached Omole and turned towards the Coca-Cola industrial complex. Each turn of the wheels deepened my despair, as the events of that day underscored the corruption and inhumanity that permeated the very institution meant to uphold justice and dignity.

The truck came to an abrupt stop opposite the Coca-Cola factory. Two of the policemen stepped out and approached the back gate of the truck, where I was locked in. Fear coursed through my mind; I was, however, somewhat reassured by the bustling environment. The area was densely populated with shops, and people moved about attending to their daily business. I was ordered to step down from the truck. I hesitated, questioning their intentions. One possibility crossed my mind: perhaps they were heading to Alausa Police Station opposite the Lagos State Secretariat. However, I refused their command and insisted that I would accompany them to their office. I wanted to ensure other officers could witness the state of my clothing, the injuries on my body, and the events I had experienced, documented in a statement I could sign.

To my shock and dismay, one of the policemen responded coldly. 'Wait for me,' he said before returning to the truck cabin. Moments later, he emerged with a rifle. He pointed it at me and declared, 'If you don't come down now, I will kill you, and nothing will happen.' Terrified and with thoughts of *accidental discharges* dominating the headlines of daily newspapers, I reluctantly stepped out of the truck. As soon as I complied, the pickup truck veered off, its occupants roaring with laughter as they drove away. In the state I was left, I could not return to the office. My appearance was humiliating–I looked like a labourer who had just finished a gruelling shift of cement mixing at a construction site. The policemen neither asked how I would get back to where I had come from nor whether I had money for transportation.

When wielded responsibly, power is a divine tool meant to improve lives, build infrastructure, and promote welfare. But absolute power, exercised without the fear of God or consideration for life's unpredictable nature, becomes a weapon of misuse. That day, I was reminded of how such power could degrade rather than uplift. When I eventually got home, my wife was alarmed. The dishevelled state in which I arrived was far from how I had left that morning, and my early return was unusual. Exhaustion from the beating and the truck's deliberately rough driving left me unable to return to work that day. My job would have to fend for itself as I struggled to recover. Some might criticise me for meddling in matters that did not concern me. I understand that perspective, but I attribute it to ignorance. The Bible teaches us to look out for one another's welfare. A nation cannot persist in such a callous manner without voices speaking up for the downtrodden. Figures like the late Gani Fawehinmi and Femi Falana stand as testaments to this duty. They have risked their lives to uphold the dignity of the oppressed, ensuring that the voiceless are heard. Their courage is a beacon for those who believe in justice, and their example reminds us that someone must stand for the poor and the broken in our society.

CHAPTER TEN

EQUALITY BEFORE THE LAW

When the Constitution of Nigeria was drafted in 1914 by the British colonial authorities, we were led to believe that it guaranteed equal rights for all citizens under the law. However, the experiences of many individuals have disproven this idealised principle. In reality, those with connections in the upper echelons of society enjoy the lion's share of these so-called rights, while the less privileged often bear the brunt of systemic inequities. The Nigerian Police Force (NPF) is a glaring example of this disparity. At crime scenes, officers often display undue reverence for individuals of high social standing, offering them military salutes and deference. Figures addressed as *Chief this or Chief that* frequently escape scrutiny, even when implicated. Evidence that an untrained investigator could identify and present in a court of law is often ignored deliberately when such influential figures are involved.

In stark contrast, innocent bystanders–unconnected to the crime in any meaningful way–can find themselves arrested and detained. These detentions are not merely a matter of days but can extend into weeks, months, or even years. The decisive factor is not guilt or innocence but the detainee's social connections and the financial resources of their friends or family. Without someone influential enough to navigate the *system* or provide the necessary bribe to secure their release, these individuals are left to languish. This systemic injustice has plunged countless innocent people into cycles of perpetual poverty and obscurity. Many are snatched from their workplaces or trades simply for being in the wrong place at the wrong time, and they remain in illegal detention for years. Their plight is compounded by the absence of advocates with the requisite *timber and calibre* to influence the enforcement hierarchy. The result is a justice system that is far removed from its foundational promise of equality, disproportionately punishing the powerless while shielding the privileged.

People are often arrested and detained for incidents that do not warrant such actions, particularly in cases of motor accidents. In such situations, the individuals who primarily need to be interviewed are the drivers of the vehicles involved, regardless of the severity of the accident–provided that no lives were lost. These drivers are expected to give statements to the police regarding the cause of the incident, typically to officers at the scene. At most, the driver might be taken to the police station to formalise their statement and sign it. In such cases, the police may require a reputable guarantor to assure that the individual will appear when summoned. Failure to present the suspect could result in the forfeiture of any property signed as a guarantee. This process should suffice to ensure compliance without the need for unwarranted detention.

Under the principles of justice, offenders and suspects–both of whom are presumed innocent until proven guilty–should only be detained if absolutely necessary. Cases should be fully investigated, and the findings documented in comprehensive written recommendations. These recommendations should then be submitted to the public prosecution service for review. The prosecution must determine whether the evidence supports a strong case in court and whether pursuing the matter serves the public interest. This systematic approach ensures that justice is upheld while minimising unnecessary detentions and respecting the rights of individuals involved in such incidents.

It is always amusing, yet tragic, to observe how people would flee the moment they spotted uniformed policemen or police vans approaching a crime scene. Even those who had been going about their normal routines in the area when the incident occurred–often the ones with first-hand knowledge of what transpired–would scatter. These people, who could have provided crucial information about the events, the people involved, and the sequence of actions, avoided any interaction with the enforcement agents. Their fear was deeply ingrained: they wished to avoid being implicated, detained, or scapegoated, which could lead to the loss of their freedom, the disruption of their livelihoods, and the suffering of their families.

In Nigeria, testifying to the police as a witness is often a perilous decision. Good citizenship could lead to dire consequences, including assassination or brutal attacks. These reprisals typically occurred either at the victim's home under the cover of night or in public, sometimes even in the presence of family and friends. A chilling example of this reality was widely reported in a national daily newspaper, highlighting the dangers of cooperating with law enforcement. The story involved a developing community plagued by relentless armed robberies, both day and night. One landlord in the area, suspected of leading one of the gangs, was reported to the police by another resident. Hoping to make the neighbourhood safer, the resident went to the station and formally reported his suspicions about the landlord. The officers, including the Divisional Police Officer (DPO), received him warmly, praised his courage, and urged him to document and sign his statement, assuring him it would aid their investigation. Unaware of the risks, the resident complied.

The suspect was promptly arrested and questioned. However, being a seasoned criminal, he manipulated the system and obtained a photocopy of the signed statement implicating him. How this document came into his possession remains unclear, but it was evident that someone within the police force facilitated the breach, with or without the DPO's knowledge or consent. Two months later, the consequences of this breach unfolded in a devastating attack. Late at night, the whistle-blower's house was besieged by a gang of assailants, who arrived in a bus packed with armed men. The scale and aggression of the attack resembled a militant operation. The gang destroyed the compound's gate, and the deafening sound of gunfire served as a stark warning for neighbours to stay indoors if they valued their lives. Some neighbours attempted to call the emergency services, but for reasons unknown, help did not arrive until two hours after the attackers had vanished.

During the attack, the gang dismantled the house's strong iron gate and stormed inside. Despite his wife's desperate attempt to hide him in the toilet, the intruders ransacked the entire home, eventually finding him. They delivered what they considered *ultimate justice*, savagely beating him to death and riddling his body with approximately 20 bullets. To further punish the family, they shot his wife in both legs, leaving her critically injured with the intent of crippling her for life. This tragic incident exposed the fatal consequences of trying to do the right thing in a deeply flawed system. It underscored the pervasive mistrust in law enforcement and the harsh realities faced by those who dared to seek justice in a society where corruption and criminality often overshadowed the rule of law.

Every day, the headlines of our glossy newspapers are dominated by stories of politicians accused of misappropriating government funds or bank directors who have embezzled billions of naira. Before the Economic and Financial Crimes Commission (EFCC) even takes such individuals into custody for investigation, prominent lawyers with the highest legal titles begin competing fiercely to represent the alleged suspects. These legal professionals are drawn not only by the potential prestige but also by the substantial financial compensation expected should they secure the client's freedom through the courts. The race to apply for bail begins in earnest, with every legal tactic and argument from their arsenals being deployed to win custody rights for their high-profile clients.

On 8 October 2012, during the NTA news bulletin and on Ben TV, I was stunned to see Mr Lawan, the chairman of the Petroleum Subsidy Investigation Committee, at the House of Representatives. Despite being reportedly suspended by the chamber, he was visibly active, contributing to discussions on political issues. This raised a perplexing question in my mind: does the House of Representatives have a different interpretation of the term *suspension* from that which is generally applied in civil service establishments? In its conventional sense, as understood within civil service frameworks, *suspension* means being temporarily relieved of one's position. This can take different forms–suspension with full salary, with half-pay, or, in cases of severe misconduct, without any salary at all. The purpose of suspension is to allow an investigation or inquiry to proceed without interference while affording the individual the benefit of the doubt. If found not guilty, the person can return to their position with their reputation restored. However, in Mr. Lawan's case, despite allegations of serious misconduct, he seemed to continue engaging in public affairs as if the suspension held no tangible consequence.

The allegations against Mr Lawan were grave. His committee had reportedly omitted the names of certain petroleum companies implicated in the subsidy scam. It was widely speculated that these omissions were not accidental but deliberate acts following significant financial inducements in the form of thousands of US dollars. This situation prompts the pressing question: who, exactly, is fooling whom in this country? Who is deceiving whom, and at what cost to the nation's integrity? Equally noteworthy are the numerous cases involving politicians investigated for various fraudulent activities. Investigators often unearth substantial evidence to prosecute them, yet once these individuals are granted bail by the courts, the cases frequently vanish from public discourse. The trillions of naira illicitly acquired through the privilege of their political positions remain unaccounted for, leaving the public disillusioned and justice unfulfilled.

I recall reading about a man who became disabled, not by an act of God but by the enactment of a law. A state governor imposed Sharia law on his citizens, establishing Sharia courts that decreed amputations–hands, legs, or both–for crimes such as stealing a meagre sum of money, a mobile phone, or a purse. Ironically, during the same governor's tenure, he allegedly stole trillions of naira. Yet, the judiciary found no grounds to hold him accountable, let alone subject him to the punitive measures he imposed on others. Such hypocrisy reflects the double standards ingrained in the system.

When Gbenga Daniel's father passed away, it was rumoured that an exorbitant amount was spent on his funeral–on the hearse, the coffin, and the ceremonies surrounding his burial. Despite the allegations and investigations surrounding his tenure as governor of Ogun State, particularly accusations of embezzling the state's treasury, he paraded himself in public without a hint of remorse. Such ostentatious displays of wealth, in the face of damning allegations, speak volumes about the lack of accountability in the country.

While I am an advocate of freedom of expression and support individuals' rights to spend their wealth as they see fit, public ethics must be honoured, respected, and upheld. A person accused of plundering state resources should exhibit the dignity to challenge and disprove such accusations rather than flaunt wealth that raises further suspicions. In a developed nation, such grandiose displays could prompt public inquiries into the individual's tenure. Yet, Nigeria remains a peculiar case–a nation seemingly designed to enable a select few to monopolise its wealth while leaving ethical accountability by the wayside.

CHAPTER ELEVEN
WONDERS OF NIGERIA

There are no specific laws or regulations stating that when a crime is committed, and no individual can be directly identified as the perpetrator, law enforcement must refrain from taking action. In such cases, if no one can be pinpointed at the scene as the offender, law enforcement agents, such as the police, may resort to what is termed *mass arrest*. This entails apprehending individuals present at or near the scene of the crime, particularly if they fail to provide information or identify the suspected perpetrator.

Mass arrests are typically employed to facilitate thorough searches, interrogations, and, where necessary, DNA analyses. These procedures aim to uncover any criminal records or evidence of involvement. Such examinations are conducted at the police station. Following these investigations, individuals found to have no connection to the crime are usually released without charges and permitted to resume their normal activities. However, for those whose backgrounds reveal prior offences, connections to the case, or implicating evidence from others, more than 24 hours of detention may be warranted. This additional time allows for a thorough forensic examination of evidence collected at the scene. In cases where a direct or indirect link to the crime is established, law enforcement agencies, such as the police, Department of State Services (DSS), or Independent Corrupt Practices and Other Related Offences Commission (ICPC), must seek a court-granted special licence to extend custody beyond the initial 24-hour period.

Nigeria, however, operates uniquely among nations. As a friend often remarks during our conversations about Nigeria's political, social, moral, leadership, and legal attitudes, he frequently makes an observation that never fails to elicit laughter: 'When God created that country', he would say, 'He made them a unique people in distinct locations, geographically close yet vastly different. He gave each region unique abilities and resources suited for their development. The North, with its arid desert, flourished in its way. The South, blessed with rainforests and fertile land, prospered too. Each tribe was endowed with distinct cultures and traditions, with little in common, including religion. But then the British came. For their selfish interests, they sowed seeds of hatred among the tribes, uniting them forcefully and diplomatically into one country under a centralised government. This displeased God. In His anger, He stripped the regions of their prosperity and pride, qualities they had once cherished. He removed the virtues of good leadership from their religious books, leaving them adrift. That is why, instead of moving forward, the country seems to move in reverse.'

Though spoken with a touch of humour, this sentiment captures the complexities and frustrations often associated with Nigeria's struggles, shedding light on the interplay of history, governance, and societal challenges. I have reflected deeply on my friend's emphatic observations, and I must admit that I found no aspect of the analogy to dispute or dismiss. Perhaps only politicians could raise criticisms or offer denials of these claims. Politicians, by nature, have a unique way of viewing situations, often far removed from the perspective of ordinary citizens.

Our rule of law and its implementation is starkly different from what is obtainable in other nations. The oft-repeated assertion, 'We are making progress, and we shall soon be there', serves merely as a tool to pacify the masses–an attempt to instil patience with the promise of a better future that remains perpetually out of reach. But are politicians truly living the same reality as the average citizen? Do the laws and law enforcement agents treat everyone equally? Yes, we may all claim to shop in the same markets–be it supermarkets, malls, or public open markets–but our choices are undoubtedly shaped by the weight or lightness of our wallets. The price of a bag of rice fluctuates unpredictably, like children playing with a *yo-yo*. Discussing the prices of soup ingredients or stew components would only compound the frustration. And what of petrol and kerosene for generators and cooking? Can we ignore the injustice of unequal electricity supply that leaves some houses in darkness while others bask in uninterrupted light? Electricity here behaves like an untamed sea–erratic and stormy–offering no stability or comfort.

While we understand that issues like herders and banditry have kept farmers from their fields, what about the police and military checkpoints? These have become little more than toll gates, where traders and transporters are forced to *deposit* money at gunpoint, with no hope of reclaiming it–let alone earning interest. These are unofficial *mini-banks,* where extortion has replaced protection. I recall an incident from several years ago, which I witnessed from the balcony of my home. A young man, a graduate from a Nigerian university, had been unable to secure his dream job, one that matched the calibre of his education. Undeterred, he decided to start small. He ventured into making liquid soap for bottle washing, a product sought after by companies like Coca-Cola and Seven-Up for cleaning reusable bottles.

On his way back to his rented workshop with the chemicals needed for production, he was stopped by the police. Unable to meet their usual demands for payment, he signalled them to follow him to his workshop to verify his legitimacy. In what could only be described as a farcical show of force, two police vans followed his hired pickup as though escorting a governor or commissioner on official duty. Upon arrival at the site, the police demanded he accompany them to their station. Realising the futility of compliance, knowing they would likely seize his products, his rented pickup, and perhaps even detain him indefinitely, he refused. Neighbours, drawn by the commotion, gathered to appeal to the officers. Instead of acting with honour, the senior officer threatened to arrest the bystanders if they did not mind their business. The scene was nothing short of disgraceful–a ridiculous and unimaginable display of power abuse.

Fortunately, the young man had a connection–a senior police officer whom he promptly called. Handing the phone to the lead officer at the scene, the tide quickly turned. Within five minutes, the senior officer was overheard meekly responding, 'Yes, sir. Yes, sir'. Out of shame and wounded pride, the police left the site empty-handed, abandoning their pursuit. This incident, like many others, underscores the glaring inequalities and systemic failures within our society. The very institutions meant to serve and protect have, far too often, become tools of oppression and exploitation.

Imagine if that young man had not known someone within the hierarchy; his business could have been ruined, leaving his employees jobless and their families plunged into hardship due to the sudden loss of income from their breadwinners. He might have languished in a police cell for months or years without having committed any offence. Allow me to take my readers on a thorny journey through the harrowing experiences of two Nigerians, whose cases were widely reported in the national newspapers. One such case was that of Mr Lukman Adeyemi, a bricklayer. Out of sheer generosity and kindness–similar to the situation I experienced with the theft of my Beetle car–Adeyemi temporarily provided accommodation to a fellow bricklayer friend who had been out of work for some time. This friend, in turn, knew another group of bricklayers who had hired a woman to fetch water for a construction site. Tragically, the woman was murdered, likely as part of a suspected ritual killing.

When the bricklayers were arrested, they implicated Adeyemi's friend during police interrogation, falsely naming him as an accomplice. The police summoned Adeyemi's friend for questioning, and out of goodwill, Adeyemi accompanied him to the station. Confident of his friend's innocence, he intended to vouch that his friend had been working with him on the day of the incident–a disappearance that had already become a much-discussed topic in the community. Shockingly, both Adeyemi and his friend were arrested and detained for a crime that neither concerned nor connected them. Their ordeal spiralled into an unimaginable nightmare: the two men were held in correctional facilities for a combined total of nine years before being transferred to prison, where they endured an additional 20 years of incarceration. This totalled 29 agonising years of wrongful imprisonment for a crime they neither committed nor had any knowledge of. Under duress, they were coerced by officers of the Special Anti-Robbery Squad (SARS) into confessing to the crime. Their false confession was the cornerstone of the case against them.

It was only thanks to the diligence and compassion of a prison welfare officer, Mr Awesu, that their story began to change. Mr Awesu listened to their accounts and reached out to a charity organisation, the Centre for Justice and Mercy, led by Pastor Hezekiah Oluyemi. The organisation took up the case and, through persistent legal advocacy, succeeded in securing the men's release through due court processes. Their story is a sobering reminder of the flaws in the justice system and the devastating consequences of neglecting fairness and due process.

In Nigeria, the mistreatment of the underprivileged by those entrusted with their protection remains a troubling phenomenon. It seems there is no end to the injustices suffered by the poor at the hands of those trained and empowered by the government to safeguard lives and property. One particularly heart-breaking case is that of Mr Kazeem Adesina, who spent 15 years in a correctional facility without ever being charged or tried for any offence. It was only through the intervention of Justice Oyindamola of the Lagos High Court, Ikeja, that an *unconditional release* was ordered. The case was championed by Counsel Abraham, who filed a suit against the Lagos State Attorney General, the Commissioner of

Police, and the Controller of the Nigerian Correctional Service in Lagos State.

Miscarriages of justice are, sadly, not unique to Nigeria. Around the world, innocent individuals have been wrongfully detained, imprisoned, or sent to correctional facilities. In the United States, for example, cases of racial injustice often result in innocent individuals–particularly black men–being convicted while the true perpetrators become crown witnesses against them. One man was released after spending over 40 years in prison for a crime he did not commit. Similarly, in the United Kingdom, individuals have been wrongfully imprisoned for years, only to be exonerated later. These cases underscore a global issue: the fallibility of justice systems.

What sets the Nigerian experience apart, however, is the glaring lack of accountability and reparation for those who have been wrongfully imprisoned. The absence of compensation for years lost in detention, for the physical and psychological suffering endured, or for the socioeconomic damage inflicted is a stark indictment of the system. Where do we begin to quantify the losses? Consider the lives derailed by these wrongful detentions: the income lost from jobs or businesses left behind, the irreparable damage to family structures, and the societal stigma attached to imprisonment. Many lose their properties, sold off in their absence, while some find their wives have remarried in their prolonged absence. The psychological toll of such experiences lingers, not only for the individual but also for their children, whose lives are irreversibly altered. The larger question remains: what justice can be offered to those who have suffered so deeply and for so long? Without adequate reparations and a commitment to reform, the cycle of injustice threatens to persist, leaving countless others to fall victim to a broken system.

In the United States of America, when a person is finally freed from prison after being wrongfully convicted, they are compensated with millions of dollars to help them rebuild their lives from scratch. Similarly, in the United Kingdom, there is a principle of compensating those who were unlawfully imprisoned. A notable example is the children of the first generation of West Indians who arrived in the United Kingdom on the ship *Windrush* in the early 1950s. Despite being born in the United Kingdom, many of these children were wrongfully denied citizenship and, in some cases, forcibly repatriated to the Caribbean. However, when lawyers challenged these injustices in court, many of these individuals were vindicated. They were flown back to the United Kingdom at government expense, granted significant monetary compensation in sterling, and received unreserved apologies for the miscarriage of justice, including formal statements of regret from the Prime Minister in office at the time of the court rulings.

Nigeria must step out of the shadows of primitivism and join the community of enlightened nations. The cases of individuals like Lukman Adeyemi and Kazeem Adesina are not isolated; countless others have had their lives destroyed by the actions of security agencies. These individuals deserve substantial monetary compensation for the denial of their freedom, unlawful detention in prisons or so-called rehabilitation centres, and unjust incarceration in police custody. As highlighted in this book, many languish in these facilities, reduced to skeletal figures–85 per cent bone and 15 per cent flesh. Among them are the innocent and those guilty of minor infractions, such as stealing small amounts of money or a mobile phone to afford a single meal. Shockingly, some have been detained for over 15 years without formal trial or a court hearing.

While the current Minister of Interior of Nigeria, Dr Olubunmi Tunji-Ojo, has been praised for his transformative work at the Passport Issuance Office, including expediting the release of backlogged passports, this momentum must extend to the justice system. Citizens should not be abandoned to rot in detention at the hands of the police and other security agencies. How many people have died in custody, their families left in the dark? How many suffer daily in inhumane conditions, with no sanitation, no medical care, and inadequate food? We are all human beings and citizens of this country. The system must treat every individual with dignity and respect, recognising their humanity and rights. It is time to ensure that justice, fairness, and compassion prevail in the Nigerian criminal justice system.

CHAPTER TWELVE

MY DILEMMA OF THE NEW MINIMUM WAGE OF ₦70,000

Sometimes, I find myself wondering about the root of our problems in this country called Nigeria. It often appears as though some of our leaders speak before they think, as though this impulsiveness is a mark of their superiority. To them, freedom of speech seems to equate to a display of power–an assertion that they are beyond challenge in a court of law. Their reasoning seems to rest on the idea that, as senior figures in the law-making process, they know the law better than anyone else. We are all aware that many of today's political leaders lack both reputation and integrity, rendering them undeserving of the positions they hold. When one dares to criticise their actions or highlight their deliberate misdeeds, they and their unruly supporters often retort that their positions are divinely ordained, claiming, 'It is the act of God that brought us here.'

Recently, the Federal Government approved a new minimum wage of ₦70,000 for workers. For this, we must commend the

President for addressing the matter promptly–a stark contrast to his predecessors, under whose administrations such a decision could have taken three to five years of endless debates and negotiations. However, it is important to note that this minimum wage should primarily benefit the unions that negotiated it and those organisations reaping substantial profits from Nigeria's economy. It is generally understood that the increase will be applied across all employment grade levels on a percentage basis.

The nation appreciates the maturity and understanding demonstrated by the National Labour Congress and other unions, who stepped down their initial demands–from ₦470,000 to ₦250,000–before diplomatically settling on the agreed minimum wage. This peaceful resolution, avoiding nationwide strikes and public demonstrations, deserves recognition. Kudos to all those involved in the negotiations. The swift passage of the minimum wage bill through the Senate, complete with expedited debates and approval, is highly commendable. It demonstrates that the executive and legislative arms of government can collaborate effectively on issues of national importance, a promising indicator for our democratic process.

However, there are some areas of serious concern regarding the new minimum wage approval, which I hope the President's spokespersons can clarify. These concerns warrant attention to ensure the policy is not only effective but also equitable in its implementation.

1. No approved increase in the minimum wage can be truly meaningful or serve its intended purpose if the government cannot regulate the prices of essential commodities,

especially staple food items sold in local markets and supermarkets. Historically, whenever news of a minimum wage hike emerges, traders, transport operators, and property owners typically respond by increasing the prices of goods and services. This renders the wage increase ineffective for the workers it was meant to benefit. For instance, the challenges faced by the working class after the Udoji Awards of 1972 highlight this dilemma. To ensure the effectiveness of any wage increase, the government must adopt measures to regulate the cost of essential commodities, transportation, rent, and similar expenses. Without such intervention, employers may resort to laying off workers to offset the financial strain, undermining the very purpose of the wage increase.

2. Moreover, there are reports that some state governors have not yet complied with the previous minimum wage of ₦30,000, with some still paying the outdated rate of ₦18,000. The question remains: how will these governors be compelled to implement the newly approved wage of ₦70,000? This unresolved issue raises concerns about the feasibility of enforcing the new policy across all states.

3. Thirdly, the President of the Senate, Godwin Akpabio, in his exuberance over the swift passage of the minimum wage legislation, made a statement that has been interpreted as politically naïve by some observers. He suggested that the new wage should apply universally to all employees, regardless of the nature of their jobs. This interpretation has caused confusion and concern among ordinary Nigerians. Akpabio implied that even private individuals employing domestic staff, such as maids, should pay them the ₦70,000 minimum wage.

4. By extending the scope of the minimum wage law to include domestic workers, Chief Godwin Akpabio appears to have ignited further challenges for ordinary Nigerians. This interpretation adds unnecessary pressure to a system already strained by economic disparities. It is worth questioning how many union leaders themselves could afford to pay ₦70,000 to their domestic staff, were it not for the allowances and privileges associated with their positions. Rather than alleviating the struggles of the working class, such statements risk exacerbating the financial challenges faced by everyday citizens.

As I recently shared in my *Food for Thought* reflections, power often causes some individuals to become overly proud, assuming their authority is absolute and their words are beyond question. This misguided belief is often the precursor to their downfall. In matters of compensating maids and domestic workers, it is essential to base payments on what one can genuinely afford and on the local economic realities. Many of these workers receive free accommodation, meals, and even clothing from their employers. While this may not excuse inadequate pay, it reflects the practicalities of mutual support in some households.

Unlike members of the Senate or House of Representatives, who earn undisclosed salaries and allowances, the average worker does not have the luxury of extravagant income. For many, the idea of paying a maid or domestic worker ₦70,000 is impractical when that sum may represent their entire monthly salary. Fairness should guide both compensation and expectations, ensuring that dignity and mutual respect remain central in these relationships.

PART TWO

MY DETENTION EXPERIENCE IN THE UNITED KINGDOM

CHAPTER THIRTEEN

LONDON, HERE I COME!

In December 1995, I went on my annual leave from the airline. Before leaving the office, I instructed my secretary to type up my letter of voluntary retirement. However, I requested that the letter remain undated, allowing me the option to return to duty if things did not go as planned. I signed the letter and attached a signed cheque covering three months' salary in lieu of notice. When I eventually decided not to return to Nigeria Airways as anticipated, I directed my secretary to submit the letter along with the cheque to the management on my behalf. In 1995, I decided to relocate to the United Kingdom. At the time, my second wife–having legally divorced my first wife in 1983–was expecting our son. The choice to leave was far from easy, but it felt necessary. I needed to carve out a path that could secure the future I envisioned for my children.

It has never been easy for a man to leave his fatherland and emigrate to another. Various factors may contribute to such a decision, often forming in people's minds over the years. Nigeria was once a peaceful country where political differences, though creating tension at the federal level, did not overshadow the pride each region had in its distinct identity. Regional political leaders were revered and seen as almost angelic figures within their domains. Consider the Western Region, led by Chief Obafemi Awolowo, whose unprecedented achievements in infrastructural development as the Premier of Western Nigeria remain legendary. In the Eastern Region, Dr Nnamdi Azikiwe stood as a pillar of political influence, ultimately becoming the President of the Republic of Nigeria. Moving north, one cannot discuss Nigeria's political history without mentioning Sir Ahmadu Bello, a name inseparable from the region's legacy. The phrase *Ranka dede* became a near-national salutation, echoing across the country and almost earning a place in the Guinness Book of Records. Lastly, to recount Nigeria's political evolution without acknowledging Alhaji Tafawa Balewa, the dignified statesman celebrated internationally as *the voice of Africa*, would be incomplete. All these figures, now of blessed memory, either passed naturally or were victims of military coups that reshaped the nation's governance.

Man, created in the image of the Lord, was endowed with all he needs to survive. Yet, humanity is incomplete without challenges–whether facing or making them. This intrinsic struggle gave rise to the concept of *conformism*. Imagine if God had created our ten fingers as separate entities before attaching them to the hand. Such a scenario would surely spark competition among them for dominance or supremacy. If discord can arise within a single hand, how much more within a man, who may feel restless or dissatisfied despite the riches and comfort surrounding him in a specific place?

This brings us to the domain of marriage. A man meets a cultured, beautiful woman. He admires her, and their acquaintance blossoms into friendship, then courtship, allowing them to understand each other better. Eventually, they decide to unite in marriage, a commitment sealed with God's blessings, including the gift of children–sons and daughters. This is what we call a *complete family*. However, over time, challenges may arise. For one reason or another, the man or woman might engage in external relationships with someone of the opposite sex. This divergence signals that something has gone amiss–perhaps a loss of affection, interest, or admiration that once bound them together. Neither partner may pinpoint exactly when or why their love, nurtured over many years, began to fade. Such is the complexity of human relationships and the passage of time.

People do not leave one job for another merely because they feel underappreciated in terms of salary increments or overdue promotions, nor due to any signs of hostility from colleagues. Rather, they often reach a point in life where they feel they have arrived at a crossroads and must decide which path to take to fulfil their ambitions and deepest desires. Curiosity, an integral part of human development, can ignite within the spirit, persisting until it is acted upon. Consider another scenario: a young man is happily settled in his parents' home. He has a room of his, which he can decorate to his taste without needing permission. His parents do not question his freedoms, and he enjoys a sense of autonomy. However, a time may come when he begins to question his purpose. He might ask himself whether he is contributing meaningfully to his life or benefiting his parents. If he has younger siblings, he may ponder whether he serves as a good role model. Eventually, he might decide that it is time to leave the comfort of his parent's home, perhaps to allow his younger siblings the same opportunities to thrive as he once enjoyed. This realisation acts as a trigger, a turning point from which he begins to see and hear reminders that it is time to move on. The notion that he has outlived his usefulness in his parents' home takes root. From this perspective, life is never static. It evolves, either voluntarily or through circumstances that compel change, prompting shifts in one's attitudes, environment, and way of life.

The Yoruba people, known for their close-knit familial and communal ties, exemplify this principle in their cultural upbringing. In my youth, we were taught to prioritise the welfare of our elders, no matter the distance separating us from our family members. A young man or woman who saw an elderly person carrying a load on their head–a traditional method of transporting heavy items–would instinctively relieve the elder of their burden, carrying it to their home or destination.

Children were strictly instructed to prostrate before their parents, to show respect, remaining in that position until told to rise, accompanied by prayers for blessings and divine favour. A customary Yoruba expression of blessing during those times was: 'Omo mi, pele o. Ọlọrun a gbé e niyì.' which translates to, 'My child, how are you? May God glorify you. Stand up, stand up.'

Deciding to travel abroad from Nigeria in the 1960s and 1970s was neither an easy task nor a straightforward decision. It required careful consideration of the cultural aspects one would inevitably leave behind: the warmth of family bonds, the comforting familiarity of traditional diets, and the glorious Nigerian weather. Save for the slightly chilly Harmattan season in December and the refreshing rains that cooled the land and nourished farmers' crops, the climate was a consistent delight.

These rains, while causing occasional erosion, also marked a crucial time for agriculture, particularly for cocoa harvesting, where children were often assigned specific roles in the process. The prospect of moving to an unfamiliar place demanded thorough deliberation of the potential advantages and disadvantages. What if employment opportunities were scarce? What if cultural differences proved insurmountable? What if a visa application was rejected? Contingency planning was vital.

Many factors influenced the decision to embark on such a journey. Often, it stemmed from a sense of stagnation–when life seemed to offer no further avenues for progress. When every door appeared firmly shut, and all efforts to unlock them proved futile, the desire for change left little choice but to take a leap of faith. The choice of destination, however, was shaped by various factors, some within one's control and others beyond it. Having a family member or relative abroad often served as a beacon of hope. They could provide crucial insights, offer promises of support upon arrival, and even assist with the documentation required for obtaining a travel visa. Similarly, friends who had already ventured to one's desired country could offer advice, financial assistance, and moral support. Such friends were invaluable. However, not all were so supportive; some discouraged the idea outright, adding to the mental strain of an already difficult decision.

In earlier times, job advertisements and opportunities shared through reliable publications or acquaintances helped facilitate visa applications and entry permits. However, in the modern era, relying on online information for such ventures has become increasingly risky due to the prevalence of internet scams. In the face of such challenges, faith and prayer often served as a source of hope. Trusting in God provided reassurance where human efforts seemed insufficient. With unwavering faith and commitment to the process, many found themselves overcoming seemingly insurmountable obstacles, navigating the complexities of visa applications and travel arrangements with surprising ease. Faith, in such instances, was the bridge that turned dreams into reality.

The current state of the world–marked by climate change, self-driving cars, and wars between nations claiming millions of lives, will make one wonder what the world is turning to today. The pace of change is both rapid and unpredictable. Nevertheless, one hopes that God's providence will continue to offer opportunities to those desperate to travel, and striving to achieve their ambitions. As written in *Julius Caesar*, 'Cowards die many times before their deaths; the valiant never taste of death but once. Of all the wonders that I yet have heard, it seems to me most strange that men should fear; seeing that death, a necessary end, will come when it will come.' A popular saying among religious people from where I came from is, 'If the mountain cannot go to Moses, Moses will go to the mountain'. I, for one, would never discourage anyone from embarking on an adventure, for, as the saying goes, 'Nothing ventured, nothing gained.'

In Nigeria, the situation has changed so dramatically that life has become increasingly devalued. Reports of killings for unwarranted reasons now dominate the news and television broadcasts. Kidnappings by armed groups–often referred to as herdsmen–have escalated, with ransoms ranging from ₦100 million to ₦200 million, sometimes demanded in American dollars.

Farmers can no longer safely tend to their fields, and ordinary citizens are not secure in their homes, on the streets, or while travelling in private or public vehicles. The once-enjoyable luxury of travelling by night, relaxing in buses while admiring the country's natural beauty, has been overshadowed by fear and insecurity.

The abduction of children as young as eight, alongside secondary school students, frequently features on our television and radio stations. Ransom demands now reach millions of naira or thousands of dollars. Meanwhile, the soaring cost of living has placed immense pressure on citizens. Manufacturers attribute the steep rise in prices to the removal of petrol subsidies and challenges in repatriating profits. As an example, we recently heard that Guinness Nigeria plans to exit the country, potentially leading to increased unemployment and a surge in insurgency. Ironically, the people themselves often seem to act as enemies to their fellow citizens. During the recent Muslim festival, a bag of rice sold for over ₦100,000, while rams cost upwards of ₦800,000. Reflecting on the 1972 Udoji salary increase, I recall that the prices of commodities, particularly electronics, skyrocketed by over 1,000 per cent.

While I appreciate the efforts of the Nigerian Labour Congress and other trade unions advocating for better living standards, any increase in wages tends to trigger widespread inflation. News of wage increases filters through the media, prompting traders to inflate prices in anticipation of higher purchasing power. Transport costs, in particular, consume a significant portion of workers' incomes, creating a burden that is as deep as it is widespread. In contemporary times, the younger generation has introduced a term, *Japa*, which reflects the growing desperation among Nigerians to emigrate to other countries. When one considers the rising number of Nigerian youths attending schools in neighbouring countries such as Benin, Togo, and Ghana, the magnitude of Nigeria's challenges becomes evident. Despite the existence of over 10,000 universities within Nigeria, for reasons beyond comprehension, many parents and guardians still send their wards to nearby countries, paying exorbitant school fees in foreign currencies.

This compels us to critically examine the structures underpinning every facet of our economy and society. It seems there are numerous opportunities we have overlooked or neglected that could have propelled the country to greatness. Historically, nations such as South Korea and Malaysia were once economically inferior to Nigeria in terms of GDP. Today, these countries are recognised as developed nations manufacturing cars and advanced electronic products that we now import. It is worth remembering that Malaysia once came to Nigeria to source cassava and palm oil seeds; now, they export processed *garri* and palm oil back to us as finished products.

A visit to Asian shops in the United Kingdom reveals scientifically packaged yam flour, or *elubo*, imported from India and Malaysia, neatly arranged on their shelves. This unfortunate reality suggests a lack of strategic planning and accountability, as generations of Nigerians have witnessed natural resources and revenues squandered with impunity, encouraging subsequent generations to follow suit. The United Nations Declaration of Human Rights guarantees freedom of movement, and most signatory nations, Nigeria included, have incorporated this principle into their constitutions. Consequently, while we cannot prevent Nigerians from seeking better opportunities abroad, such migration often facilitates the acquisition of valuable knowledge in science, technology, and artificial intelligence–fields that are now critical to global development.

However, what is most concerning are the harrowing reports of individuals–both young and old–dying from exhaustion and illness while attempting to cross deserts en route to Egypt, Libya, Sudan, and other Arab nations. Unscrupulous individuals masquerading as businessmen and women exploit these desperate travellers, extorting substantial sums of money with promises of better jobs and improved lives. Instead, they subject these migrants to traumatic experiences: perilous desert journeys without medical care, and many women, forced prostitution in Egypt or Saudi Arabia. Nigeria appears to be at a crossroads, hindered by both internal challenges and external barriers. We find ourselves unable to move forward or retreat. The pressing question remains: where do we go from here?

CHAPTER FOURTEEN

DENIAL OF CONSTITUTIONAL RIGHTS

The journey out of Nigeria can be harrowing, particularly for those without the means to chart the right course or the fortune of encountering a God-sent helper. Many embassies in Nigeria are aware of the resilience and determination of Nigerians, who often refuse to accept rejection or failure as final or divine will. In the past, it was even possible for someone to apply for and obtain a Nigerian passport under different surnames, especially if their application to an embassy had been denied. Furthermore, there is hardly a barrier Nigerians cannot surmount. Former U.S. President George W. Bush, during a visit to Nigeria, famously remarked about a place called Oluwole in Lagos–a street corner reputed for its notoriety, where almost anything seemed possible. In Oluwole, transactions of all sorts were said to take place: passports could be altered with new names or photographs, visas could be fabricated, and applications could be processed for those who had never stepped into a passport office. These middlemen facilitated the completion of visa forms and returned passports for their clients, all for a fee.

Desperation often leads people into the hands of those they believe can make the impossible happen. However, this desperation can turn one into a figurative slave to unscrupulous individuals. Unfortunately, not all who offer help are genuine. Many exploit even their closest relations, lacking both fear of God and any sense of shame. Their actions are driven not by a desire to assist but by a determination to compound the misery of others. They are so convincing that, in moments of despair, one may accept their assurances, even when faced with clear falsehoods. In the 1960s, 1970s, and early 1980s, travelling to countries like the United Kingdom, the United States, France, or Spain was straightforward compared to today. The arduous journeys through the Libyan desert from Niger Republic or Côte d'Ivoire were not common then. With the necessary travel documents, one could simply book a flight, depart, and arrive at their destination. However, immigration checkpoints presented a different challenge.

If immigration officials suspected any irregularities–be it a forgery in a passport or entry visa, or inconsistencies between one's story and the documents provided–the traveller would be taken to a special room for thorough questioning and searches, including their luggage. Depending on the findings, the individual might be allowed to proceed or denied entry and deported on the next available flight.

For those unwilling to return and whose deception was conclusively proven, seeking refugee status became an option. This required crafting a plausible story to justify their request for asylum. In such cases, they might be sent to an asylum camp while their application was processed by the Home Office. If they could provide credible evidence of circumstances necessitating their flight from their home country, they might be granted refugee status. This entitled them to basic survival facilities, such as limited benefits, medical treatment, and accommodation in a government-sponsored hotel.

When you find yourself at a bus stop waiting for a bus or at an underground train station awaiting a train, delays can be frustrating. If, by chance, you are with other Nigerians, they are often the ones who complain bitterly about the delay or anything that does not align with their expectations. Although I refrain from correcting their behaviour–it often leads to verbal abuse, with remarks such as 'You're one of them' or 'You've overstayed your welcome and forgotten your way back to your country'–I silently address them in my thoughts. I remind them, albeit internally, that these services they now criticise do not even exist in Nigeria. Yet, here they are, expecting them to function precisely how and when they want.

One of Nigeria's most pressing issues is the lack of a maintenance culture. We fail to repair or service infrastructure until it deteriorates catastrophically. Our public transportation system is often left in the hands of private operators who neglect routine maintenance. Despite numerous complaints, vehicles remain unrepaired, and fares are exorbitantly high. Worse still, drivers sometimes change their routes mid-journey, forcing passengers to disembark. There is no law, nor any enforcement, to hold them accountable. Travelling within Nigeria, especially from Abuja to the southwest, often feels like a dramatic ordeal.

Trucks and trailers become stranded for weeks on federal roads, leading to significant losses. Agricultural products perish during these delays, becoming unsellable. One trader lamented losing yams worth six million naira while attempting to transport them to Lagos.

The Federal Ministry of Works and other agencies ostensibly responsible for road construction and maintenance appear ineffective. Billions of naira are allocated annually for these purposes, yet there is little to show for it. Accountability is conspicuously absent, and the Minister of Works rarely provides updates or explanations regarding the ministry's performance.

Another troubling example of systemic failure is the kidnapping of schoolchildren in Kagara, Kaduna State. Initial reports claimed 287 children aged 8 to 15 were abducted. However, it was later clarified that only 137 children were kidnapped. Why did the school fail to correct its erroneous figures promptly? Were the children released voluntarily, rescued through military action, or freed after negotiations and ransom payments? The state governor could not provide clear answers to these questions during media interviews. Journalist Babatunde Kolawole Otitoju, speaking on *Journalist Hangout*, highlighted that the area surrounding the school lacked basic network facilities. Journalists had to travel back to Kaduna town to file their reports, as there was no connectivity in the area. It is disgraceful that, in 2024, with substantial revenues reportedly invested in technological development, some regions, particularly those housing schools, remain without network coverage.

The abduction itself raises further concerns. How could such a large group of children, reportedly taken on foot over four hours, escape detection or intervention? Why was no timely call for security assistance made to the military? Such lapses in communication and response require serious investigation and immediate action. From these experiences, it is clear that people often have valid and compelling reasons to emigrate to other countries. They seek places where, hopefully, their families can live peacefully; their children can attend schools where teachers can perform their duties without the fear of being kidnapped.

CHAPTER FIFTEEN

LIFE IN LONDON

London, the capital of the United Kingdom, stands as one of the most popular and populous cities in the world, renowned for its wealth, cultural diversity, religious tolerance, and industrial advancements. Viewing the city on screen, one cannot help but be captivated by its vibrant atmosphere and the freedoms afforded to its inhabitants by democratic governance. Whether depicted in media, visited in person, or glimpsed during the evening news, the city appears remarkably clean, orderly, and bustling with activity.

If you have never been to London, you might find yourself wondering why its residents are always in such a hurry, moving with the precision and urgency of soldiers on parade. My observation, though, may not align with everyone's perspective, is rooted in years of living in the city. If my conclusions were to undergo research, I believe they would be substantiated. In Nigeria, time seems to work for us—we can afford to relax and still accomplish our goals without rushing. Conversely, in the United Kingdom, and indeed much of Europe, one must chase time. This requires setting an alarm–thankfully now easily managed with mobile phones, which even schoolchildren use–to wake up and prepare for school. The British government has invested heavily in public transport, creating a system that allows one to traverse the city with relative ease. While you may need to change buses or trains during your journey, the infrastructure ensures that you will reach within a 10-15-minute walk to your destination. This efficiency is the result of careful short-, medium-, and long-term planning by the central government and the London City Council.

Another remarkable aspect of the United Kingdom is its approach to housing. Across the country, one sees rows of houses in various designs, shapes, and heights. Some are sprawling blocks of flats, rising as high as 50 storeys with multiple apartments per floor. Over time, the government offers occupants the opportunity to purchase their homes, creating a pathway to homeownership for many. Perhaps most admirable is the legal system, which ensures justice and fairness for all. If you are wronged by an individual or organisation, you can engage a solicitor to present your case and guide you through the legal process. Solicitors clearly explain your rights and advise you on how to proceed, ensuring that no one takes the law into their own hands. This adherence to "the legality of the law" underscores the country's commitment to justice.

Electricity in the United Kingdom is remarkably reliable and rarely interrupted except in cases of non-payment or scheduled maintenance. Bills can be paid conveniently online via direct debit, eliminating the need for in-person visits or meter readings, as most households now use prepayment systems. Similarly, water supply operates on a metered basis, with payments deducted automatically. In rare instances where services must be temporarily disrupted, affected households receive written notice at least a week in advance, detailing the reasons and expected duration of the outage.

In cases of unpaid bills or ignored warnings, service providers may disconnect utilities. However, even this process is handled with transparency, reflecting the organised and customer-centric approach that permeates life in the United Kingdom. It is their right to take a client to court to recover their debts. One of the first things to learn when living in the United Kingdom is the importance of humility and being prepared to adapt to the local culture. If you act inappropriately or behave in a caricatured manner, people may not confront you directly or engage in arguments. Instead, their calm demeanour often compels self-reflection.

Records in the United Kingdom are meticulously maintained in a centralised database. Traffic police officers are equipped with devices that provide instant access to a vehicle's history, including its registration, particulars, insurance details, and any significant incidents. When a police officer militarily salutes you, it is not an act of deference but a practice instilled during their training. This formal courtesy does not preclude them from taking decisive action if necessary. Should a police officer suspect you of a crime, they may read you the caution, place you in handcuffs, and transport you to the nearest station in a police vehicle. Upon arrival, they will document the alleged offence and hand over the matter to the duty officers for further investigation.

Intelligence gathering remains one of the greatest achievements of law enforcement agencies in the United States, the United Kingdom, and other European countries. Their philosophy emphasises the prevention of crime as much as possible rather than focusing solely on post-crime resolution. Citizens are encouraged to provide credible information to the police, with their identities strictly protected. In cases involving serious crimes such as murder, drug trafficking, or terrorism, informants are often granted police protection to shield them from retaliation by those they report.

I recall a specific incident from the 1970s in Clapham Common, South West London, that underscores this culture of vigilance. There was a long row of one-storey flats, primarily housing elderly residents. The curtains on the windows and doors were often drawn, affording privacy to the occupants. One afternoon, a fight broke out between two men on the street. Tragically, one of the men was stabbed, collapsing on the ground, while the assailant fled the scene. In such situations, it is unwise to intervene in the altercation as a bystander. Attempting to mediate can result in being injured or misunderstood as siding with one of the parties. Returning from school at the time, I kept my distance, mindful not to interfere or risk implicating myself in the event. Mobile phones were not yet commonplace, so communication relied on landlines.

As I observed from a safe distance, I noticed an elderly resident discreetly pulling back their curtain, jotting down notes with a pen and paper. Their notes likely included details of the incident, descriptions of the individuals involved, and the time of the occurrence. Within minutes, the sound of sirens heralded the arrival of police and an ambulance, which approached swiftly, disregarding the usual one-way traffic rules. I suspected the elderly resident had used the emergency landline provided by the government to notify the authorities. From the balcony of my flat, I watched the police cordon off the area with tape and attend to the injured man, who was transported to hospital. Shortly after, two senior police officers visited the elderly resident's flat, where they remained for nearly two hours, gathering detailed information about the incident. Later in the evening, additional officers returned to collect further details, including a description of the fleeing suspect, which would likely be cross-referenced with their database to aid in identification. This incident highlights the resourcefulness of the British Metropolitan Police, who often rely on detailed observations from diverse sources, including elderly residents in housing complexes. Their systematic approach to intelligence gathering plays a critical role in combating all forms of crime effectively across the country.

CHAPTER SIXTEEN

RELOCATING MY CHILDREN TO LONDON

Everything in life has a finite span. There is always a beginning, and whether we like it or not, there must inevitably be an end. We are born on a specific day, and just as we begin our journey, there will come a moment when we must disembark at our destined stop–be it a metaphorical bus stop or an airport. This inevitability is something human beings must accept, as it is an unchangeable fact of existence. The true uncertainty lies in how the termination of life will occur. While we all hope to live long, fruitful lives–perhaps beyond a hundred years–and enjoy the rewards of our labours, this may not align with God's ultimate plan for us. Those who die in their mother's wombs or before reaching the age of fifty certainly did not choose such a fate, yet the divine design must unfold as intended.

The manner of death varies widely and often occurs under mysterious circumstances: incurable illnesses, accidents involving aircraft, motor vehicles, or motorcycles, and even unforeseen mishaps like falls while walking along roads or within the safety of one's bathroom. Death, as Shakespeare aptly put it, is a necessary end that will come when it will come. Consider those who die through acts of terrorism–unplanned, violent, and utterly unforeseen–or the countless individuals in Africa who die due to abject poverty, unable to afford a single nutritious meal for themselves or their families. The global population continually grows through births, yet it diminishes just as steadily through deaths, not all of which are attributable to natural causes. Reflecting on my personal experiences, I recall when I was employed in an organisation in Nigeria where recruitment processes were largely perfunctory. Job advertisements, candidate selection, qualification checks, and interviews appeared to adhere to laid-down procedures. However, these steps were often mere formalities to justify the appointment of a preselected candidate–someone favoured by those in authority.

The chosen candidate's name would be included in the list of interviewees. However, when assessed by a neutral interviewer, they might fall short of the required merit, especially if more qualified and competent candidates were present. Despite this, in Nigeria, merit often holds little weight in the decision-making processes of leaders. When someone other than their favoured candidate is selected, management might resort to various tactics to frustrate the individual's efforts and contributions to their assigned duties. However, unforeseen circumstances sometimes arise, enabling others to enforce fairness or adhere to the organisation's established procedures. In such rare cases, luck plays its part, allowing a deserving individual to secure an opportunity that might otherwise have been out of reach.

With all the man-made challenges confronting people in their workplaces, my mind was not completely at ease with the job assigned to me. Many of my friends, whose families lived in the United Kingdom, chose to resign from their positions once they had completed ten years of service. However, my spirit always urged me to follow my God-given desire to serve the company for fifteen years, the mandatory period outlined in the government circular for pension eligibility. Glory be to God–He guided and protected me in my work, shielding me from the schemes of enemies determined to see me fail in fulfilling the Lord's directive. As time passed, I looked back and, by the grace of God, could no longer see my adversaries; they had been vanquished, swept away as if by an earthquake from heaven. When I finally decided to retire in 1995, I drafted a letter of resignation and had my secretary prepare it, deliberately leaving out the date. This omission was intentional, giving me the flexibility to return to work if circumstances did not unfold as planned. By the time I left Nigeria on 26 December 1995, I had completed 16 years of service. I was confident in my entitlement to pension benefits, as stipulated by civil service regulations unless a new policy had altered the rules governing my legitimate rights. My home, however, was not without its challenges. My second wife was pregnant, which deeply concerned me as I worried about how she would cope alone, particularly with the daily demands of caring for our young children. I have always been reluctant to hire domestic help, given the troubling stories I have heard of their misconduct. Once, we employed a housemaid, but as there was no money for her to steal and give to the person who brought her to us, she was taken back by her recruiter without notice. I had never failed to pay her wages or treated her unkindly, yet she left without warning. This experience solidified my reservations about hiring help.

Stories of housemaids poisoning their employers, attacking them with knives, or committing other heinous acts usually made headlines in Nigerian newspapers. I recall a report about a 16-year-old girl who murdered her employer, a university professor in Jos, Plateau State. The professor had dismissed her for stealing money, and in retaliation, the girl returned days later, armed with a sharp knife, and killed her. Such accounts further convinced me that hiring a housemaid was not a risk worth taking. While in the United Kingdom, my wife gave birth to a healthy baby boy, a joyous occasion for which we fervently thanked God. She had long prayed for a son after having daughters. Tragically, she passed away from leukaemia when the boy was just eleven months old. She had been hospitalised at the University College Hospital, Ibadan, for nearly nine months before her death. Following her passing, I relocated my family from Lagos to Ibadan, where their maternal grandmother, willing to care for the children, found it more convenient. Life in Ibadan was peaceful, and the arrangement worked well until I could organise for the children to join me in the United Kingdom. By the time they arrived in 2001, my son was five years old, and our family was reunited once more.

I thank God for His support–financially, physically, and mentally–enabling me to fund the project. The costs of paying residential immigration fees, covering the DNA test, and purchasing flight tickets were overwhelming at the time. I had to borrow money from my bank in the form of loans, and, without mincing words, my banker was both encouraging and supportive throughout the process. It is important for a borrower to repay loans promptly, as this demonstrates reliability and establishes one's worth as a good customer. Despite the financial strain, the greater challenge lay in managing the children, especially considering their attitudes and behaviours. Sadly, my children were neither accommodating nor tolerant, and they resisted guidance on how to adapt to life in a new country. A significant issue arose within the family, led by the eldest daughter, who instigated discord in the rented house. The atmosphere was often tumultuous, as the girls could neither agree amongst themselves nor show mutual respect. They lacked the willingness to cooperate or accept responsibility for their actions. In contrast, the youngest boy, who was still very young at the time, received considerable attention and care. He never complained of mistreatment. However, as time passed, circumstances changed dramatically. Once he began associating with radicalised children at school, the situation took a troubling turn.

CHAPTER SEVENTEEN
WELCOME TO SCHOOL

All children in the United Kingdom are required to attend school, typically starting at the infant age of three years. For children newly arriving from foreign countries, their class placement is often determined by their age. In Nigeria, my children attended private schools, which required the payment of substantial fees but offered the advantage of allowing them to enrol in classes aligned with their age and academic progress. My eldest daughter gained admission into a private secondary school in Ibadan at the age of ten, with boarding facilities available. The youngest daughter was in Year Two at a private secondary school in Ibadan before the family emigrated to the United Kingdom. In the United Kingdom, children of working-class families must generally be at least 12 years old to gain admission into Year One of secondary school. My youngest daughter, born in October, was already in Year One at her secondary school in Ibadan. However, upon arriving in the United Kingdom, she was only eligible to join the final year of primary school, attending from January to June, before progressing to secondary school. Children born before June in a given year are often fortunate to be placed in higher classes than those born later in the same year. This reflects the educational patterns in the United Kingdom, although wealthier families may leverage private nursery education to give their children an academic advantage extending to university. Before their mother's passing, I had already paid nursery school fees for my son, as all my children began nursery education at the tender age of one. However, as the saying goes, 'Man proposes, but God disposes.' My wife's illness took a grave turn, and she was admitted to the University College Hospital in Ibadan, where she eventually passed away. May her gentle soul rest in perfect peace. Amen.

This tragic development profoundly altered the family's plans and circumstances. My son was unable to attend the nursery school for which fees had been paid, and no refund was issued. The children were relocated to Ibadan, and the family's plans were thrown into disarray. It felt as though the world had collapsed, and a heavy darkness descended upon us. When the family eventually moved abroad, we could only take a few belongings, leaving behind much of what we owned. As stated earlier, schooling in the United Kingdom, particularly for children aged three to eighteen, is primarily determined by the child's age at the time the application for admission is submitted. The young girl initially felt uneasy with the educational procedures. However, I explained to her that she needed to adapt to the new circumstances, as we could neither alter the school regulations nor the policies of the environment in which we now found ourselves. Fortunately, over time, they began to acclimatise to their new lives. The boy, who had been calm and well-behaved at home, gradually became influenced by his peers at school. On several occasions, I received phone calls informing me that he had been required to stay behind after school hours as a consequence of disruptive behaviour or rudeness towards his teachers. This was unprecedented in my experience with his sisters, whether in Nigerian schools or those in the United Kingdom.

The most alarming incident occurred one morning when one of his older sisters accompanied him to school. Children under the age of nine are required to be escorted to school and collected afterwards. She handed him over to the teachers supervising the school gates before proceeding to her college. At approximately 10:00 a.m., I received an urgent call from the school, informing me that my son was missing and could not be located among the other pupils. The school provided no further details about what had happened. Within 30 minutes, I rushed to the school and was met by the headteacher, who ushered me into her office. While we were there, someone phoned to report that the boy had been found and was in the custody of law enforcement officers. They informed us that he would soon be escorted back to the school premises.

The account given by the law enforcement officers in the headteacher's office was so distressing that I nearly collapsed. They explained that my son had sneaked out of the school with a group of his peers without anyone's knowledge. They had gone to a shop where he attempted to emulate the actions of other boys who had previously pocketed packets of chocolates from the shelves. Unknown to him, the shopkeeper had been observing his actions on the CCTV cameras. When the shopkeeper confronted him, saying, 'What are you doing there?' and reached for the telephone to scare him off, he panicked and grabbed her hand to prevent her from making the call. After a brief struggle, he let go and attempted to flee the shop in haste. Unfortunately, he collided with the sliding glass doors, which were slow to open, damaging them in the process. This drew the attention of bystanders outside the shop, who intervened when they saw him attempting to escape. The shopkeeper then emerged and explained what had happened. The police were called, and I was informed that he had been taken to the station before eventually being brought back to the school. The entire ordeal was deeply troubling and left me grappling with a mix of disbelief and despair at how quickly circumstances had escalated.

In the presence of everyone gathered in the office–the policemen, the head teacher, and several school officials–my son asked to speak privately with the officers. They agreed and followed him outside. Upon their return, the officers informed us that my son had told them he did not wish to go home with me because he feared I would beat him. I immediately assured them that I had no intention of doing so and added that I had never beaten him in the past. My son himself confirmed this. The officers explained that, in the United Kingdom, matters involving children are taken extremely seriously. Despite my assurance, which I even offered to put in writing, they deemed it unnecessary. I was allowed to return home with the understanding that my son would remain in school until the end of the day. However, the police ultimately decided to place him in temporary accommodation at an undisclosed location for the weekend. This decision left his sister questioning me, asking what I could have possibly done to their only brother. My explanation of the situation did little to appease her or other family members. Even his sister, who had dropped him off at school that Friday morning, was puzzled about how he managed to leave the premises, given the operational fences and gates surrounding the school.

In summary, the police brought my son back to school the following Monday and escorted him home after the school day ended, accompanied by school officials. When dealing with authorities–particularly the police and social services–it is often best to remain calm and composed. Any display of anger might have led them to assume I was hot-tempered and, by extension, a threat to my son. This could have escalated to the point where they deemed it necessary to place him in foster care. Once the school officials had left my house, I refrained from questioning my son about Friday's events. It is the school's responsibility, under government mandate, to investigate such matters. I chose to let sleeping dogs lie, recognising that silence was the wisest course of action.

Life is often a mix of seeking and being sought by trouble. Sometimes, trouble seems to descend upon you uninvited, like a gift from nowhere. When disputes arise, assigning blame can become murky. They say, after all, that when you pull at a tree, its roots beneath the ground are inevitably disturbed. After two years of relative peace and tranquillity in our home, another issue arose. My son's class teacher was absent from school for a week, and a temporary replacement was assigned to cover the class. On one particular day, while en route to the school, the replacement teacher remembered that her house rent was due. This was not her first stint as a replacement teacher, but that morning, she decided to stop at a bank ATM to withdraw the required funds to settle her rent before continuing to school.

During the school break, only a few pupils were in the class. Some were chatting, while others were engrossed in discussions about their schoolwork. As a result, no one was paying attention to my son. He wandered over to the teacher's desk, took her bag, opened it, and removed almost all the cash she had withdrawn that morning from her purse. What he did with the money turned into a tale many would describe as both hilarious and reminiscent of a scripted comedy. My son suddenly became a self-appointed *Messiah*, determined to make everyone around him wealthy without any effort. He began distributing the money to his classmates, handing out £20 and £10 notes to several of them. Unfortunately, the teacher did not check her bag during the day, as she never expected anyone to tamper with it during school hours. Such an incident had never occurred before. It was not until she returned home and confidently opened her bag to pay her rent that she discovered her purse was empty. By then, the school had closed, all pupils and staff had left, and the gates were firmly secured. Deciding to keep the matter private, she resolved to address it the following day when school reopened. However, events unfolded sooner than she anticipated. One of my son's classmates, a girl who lived near us, returned home with a £20 note and handed it to her mother, explaining how she had come by the money. Alarmed, the mother immediately took her daughter back to the school to report the incident and returned the money to the headteacher, who was still on the premises.

The next day, several pupils confirmed that my son had given them money. Nearly all of them returned what they had received. By the time the teacher arrived at school to report her missing cash, the mystery had already become widely known and was the talk of the day. My son, though never a liar, sometimes acted without considering the consequences. When confronted, he admitted to his actions without hesitation. Later that day, I was invited to the school and informed of what had transpired. My first step was to visit the girl's mother after school to offer my sincere apologies for the embarrassment my son had caused her family. I also requested permission to apologise directly to the teacher, but the school authorities declined, assuring me that the matter had been handled by their regulations. Following this incident, the London Borough where we lived summoned me to numerous meetings, inquiries, and lectures, as though I were a child needing instruction on basic responsibilities. These sessions felt like an unnecessary exercise, akin to teaching someone how to cross the road safely in a bustling shopping district. Nevertheless, I had no choice but to attend, even though I found the process to be a waste of my time and an insult to my intelligence. Ironically, many of those offering me parenting advice were much younger than I was. Reflecting on the entire episode, it remains both a lesson and a source of amusement, albeit with its fair share of challenges.

They did not mention what the council policies and regulations are that have been dented the children and families of people from Africa countries in regard to their cultures and traditions. I recognised that we are in foreign country and have to live in accordance with their ways of life, but when three-year-old children were taught how to use the phone and make report of any of their parents particularly the single parents who has to jog child cares and their professional career to be able to provide the needs of their children that left miles of trauma to be admired and justified. The council failed to outline the specific policies and regulations that have adversely affected children and families of African descent, particularly regarding their cultures and traditions. I understand that living in a foreign country requires adapting to its way of life. However, teaching three-year-old children to use phones to report their parents–especially single parents who must juggle childcare and professional careers to meet their children's needs–leaves an enduring psychological toll that cannot be justified. Institutions established to protect children are, unfortunately, failing to add meaningful value to their lives. In recent years, we have witnessed an alarming rise in teenage boys engaging in violent acts, including stabbing and killing one another. In my view, the absence of strong home and parental influence plays a significant role in these tragic outcomes. Parents must be allowed to instil discipline and assign essential duties to their children at home. Proper home training would make children useful to their communities and the nation at large. Removing children from their parents and placing them in foster care is akin to pouring petrol on a raging fire–it exacerbates the challenges in their lives. While not all parents have the same level of patience or approach to raising children, family discipline remains essential. Investing in the proper upbringing of children within their families is critical for their well-being and development.

CHAPTER EIGHTEEN

PARENTING IN LONDON AS A SINGLE PARENT

I am profoundly grateful to the management of the private school my son attended. Both incidents recounted in the previous chapter occurred during his time at primary school. The school authorities must have realised that my son had lost his mother before the age of one. Consequently, it would have made little sense to expel him from the schooling system. I believe they took my situation as a single parent into account, as I had informed both the school and the local authority that his mother had passed away before he celebrated his first birthday. Although his behaviour warranted some form of strict discipline, the headteacher chose to act with remarkable empathy and wisdom. Some educators are truly God-sent, and this particular headteacher deserves commendation–a badge of honour, even–for her approach. Transitioning to secondary school, however, brought new challenges. Despite growing older and being expected to think critically before acting, his attitudes and behaviour showed no improvement. It seemed as though self-reflection and accountability were concepts absent from his philosophy. From his first year in secondary school,

I noticed a gradual decline in his behaviour. I suspect he began associating with peers from troubled backgrounds or those who disregarded their parents' guidance. He started going out as he pleased, often staying out until unreasonably late hours. When questioned about his whereabouts, he would provide neither clear nor satisfactory explanations. The school frequently called to report disruptive behaviour during lessons.

At home, I consistently tried to counsel him about the importance of education and the consequences of misconduct. I emphasised the advantages of academic success and the long-term risks of poor choices. This decline in behaviour was all the more disheartening because, during his primary school years, he had been an exceptional pupil with commendable academic achievements. He often brought home certificates of recognition for reading and other school competitions. On one occasion, he was awarded a book by J.K. Rowling, the renowned author of *The Harry Potter* series, whose captivating novels have been adapted into films. It was a proud moment that reflected his potential–a potential that I hoped to nurture and see flourish. The rate at which he was growing in height might have contributed to his assumption that my efforts to enlighten him about good behaviour for the future were unnecessary. Whenever I addressed him on these matters, he would merely smile, offering no response to my statements. Subsequently, he formed a close friendship with a schoolmate who lived near our house, though this boy was a year older than him. I had hoped their association would positively influence his attitude and behaviour, as the other boy was well-known in the area for being level-headed, serious, and ambitious.

However, the day I met the boy's mother left me speechless. She shared with me her concerns about the recent changes in her son's behaviour. According to her, since her son had started associating with mine, there had been a marked and troubling deterioration in his conduct. It was heartbreaking to hear this from a single mother raising three children alone. As a matter of urgency, she revealed that she had finalised plans to send her son to a private boarding school in Nigeria to address these issues. Her disappointment in the situation was evident in her determination to take drastic measures to safeguard her son's future. This conversation inspired me to consider a similar course of action for my son. Sending him to a reputable private boarding school in Nigeria, where I could arrange for a teacher to look after him on my behalf, seemed like a promising solution. It appeared to be a practical way to instil values and discipline that would benefit him in the future. However, when I inadvertently mentioned this plan to his sisters, seeking their support, I was disheartened by their reaction. One of them informed him of my intentions and encouraged him to resist the idea vehemently. When I confronted her about why she had interfered, she explained that she believed I would never allow him to return to the United Kingdom after completing secondary school.

During a subsequent conversation with the girls, I clarified my intentions. I explained that the purpose of sending him to Nigeria was solely to provide him with an opportunity to learn more about African culture, develop self-control, and gain better behavioural insights during his secondary education. Despite my explanations, the idea was met with resistance and ultimately abandoned before it could materialise. In the end, the other boy was sent to Nigeria, completed his schooling, and returned home a transformed young man–a son his mother could be truly proud of. In addition to the almost daily phone calls from school alerting me to my son's misbehaviour, he was often made to stay behind after school to serve various punishments or sanctions. One day, while I was resting in bed, he returned home accompanied by one of his schoolmates. Unaware of my presence, they spoke freely about the financial benefits supposedly enjoyed by children living with foster parents. The boy was telling my son that some of his friends had claimed foster children received generous allowances from Council officials, enabling them to buy whatever they desired. My son replied that he was considering how he could become a foster child and remain in that arrangement until he turned 18. I was deeply concerned about the kind of young people or groups my son was associating with, but I felt powerless due to the attitudes of his sisters.

One particularly troubling incident at school began with an argument in the cloakroom between my son and another boy. The other student accused him of associating with a group of boys who allegedly ambushed women at a local park, stole their mobile phones, and passed the stolen items to a member of the gang to sell. According to the boy, they would then split the proceeds. Enraged, my son reportedly beat the boy mercilessly and threatened to attack his family home and set it on fire. The matter was reported to the school authorities, and I was invited to a disciplinary committee meeting. Neither my son nor the other boy was present, but the committee reviewed a video recording of the incident taken by another student. The incident report was read aloud to those in attendance. As usual, all I could do was offer my unreserved apology to the school and request that they convey the same to the parents of the other boy.

I typically travel to Nigeria once a year for my annual holiday, usually for about four weeks. On one occasion, I suggested to my son that he join me for a change of environment. It seems he mentioned this to one of his sisters, who then planted the idea in his mind that I might be trying to trick him into returning to Nigeria permanently and abandoning him there. That was the end of that plan. Whenever I visit Nigeria, my relatives often ask why I haven't brought any of my children along, even one at a time. They miss them dearly, especially their maternal grandmother, who had lived with them in Ibadan during my earlier absences. However, my children's perspectives have changed; they have formed new friendships in the United Kingdom and our neighbourhood. Additionally, the news and images they see on Nigerian television fail to inspire any desire to visit our country.

CHAPTER NINETEEN

POLICE DETENTION IN THE UNITED KINGDOM

There comes a day when trouble may seek you out, no matter how God-fearing or devout you are. Even the most committed individuals are not exempt, as seen in the biblical account of Satan testing Jesus Christ. He led Jesus to the pinnacle of a mountain, urging Him to jump, and showed Him the splendour of worldly riches, promising all would be His if He would bow in worship. Some religious teachings lead us to believe that God allows such challenges to test our faithfulness and dedication. Indeed, nothing happens without God's knowledge and approval. Life itself is temporary, and so too are the events that unfold within it. Life has never been a smooth journey; like a boat at sea, it is constantly tossed by the wind, testing the competence of those steering it.

One particularly eventful day, my son went to school, and before the close of lessons, I received three separate phone calls from his teachers. They reported that he had been disruptive during lessons, caused trouble with other pupils during break and been rude to a teacher. At that moment, there was little I could do, as the calls were not invitations to visit the school but merely updates on his behaviour. That day, I was on a night shift and needed rest before returning to work in the evening. When my son came home, I did not check the time but could hear him in his room. I was in bed, dressed in my pyjamas. After some minutes, I called him into my room and asked him to sit by my side. I questioned him about the purpose of his head and whether he had a brain in his skull, as his actions were not befitting the dignity of our family within the community. Without uttering a word, he stood and walked out of the room. I heard his footsteps descending the stairs to the living room. Assuming he was going to have lunch or watch television, I thought little of it. The house fell silent, and I presumed he was reflecting on what I had said.

Approximately two hours later, loud bangs on the front door startled me, accompanied by shouts of 'Police!' The noise was so unexpected and surreal that I momentarily thought I was dreaming. I got out of bed and peered through my window to see two uniformed policemen standing at the doorstep. Before I could reach the door, they had banged it several more times, each knock heavier and more aggressive than the last. Irritated, I shouted that I was on my way down. When I opened the door, I politely asked them what they wanted and whom they were looking for. Before I could say more, one of them asked, 'Are you Mr Olatunji Olusanya?' When I confirmed that I was, they informed me they had come to arrest me. Bewildered, I asked for the reason, but they replied that I would be told at the station. I requested permission to change out of my pyjamas, and, to my relief, they allowed me to do so without objection. I returned to my room, changed into an outing dress, and came downstairs to join them in their official vehicle, which they had parked nearby. I was directed to step into the back cabin of the van. The doors were firmly shut and locked, while the two policemen took their positions in the front seats. Once again, history was repeating itself in my life. This time, however, it was in a clean, modern van, where I was the sole occupant of the back cabin.

Our first stop was the police station on Ripple Road, Barking. Interestingly, the station had since been closed and converted into a female beauty complex. The van was parked behind the building for what felt like over an hour while the officers went inside. I assumed they were briefing their colleagues about the new *criminal* they had arrested and now had in custody. I speculated that there were no vacant cells at this station, as they soon emerged and began driving again. I did not know our destination, as they were not obliged to inform me of their procedures or movements. I felt as though I had entered *Animal Farm* once again. The journey was uncomfortable, with the van bumping and jolting frequently. There was nothing to hold onto for balance, and I could not tell if the rough ride was due to the condition of the roads or if it was intentionally harsh to reinforce my status as a detainee. Eventually, the van stopped at another police station. When I was asked to step out, I looked around, but the location was unfamiliar. I had no idea where I was, as the van had passed through walled tunnels, obscuring the outside environment. Without windows, I was unable to see where I had been taken, making the journey feel like an eternity.

Upon arrival at the station, there were no signs to indicate where we were. I was led into the reception area without being handcuffed. Instead, the officers flanked me as they guided me inside. The custody procedures commenced immediately. I was searched to ensure I was not hiding any dangerous items; my belt and shoes were confiscated. The search felt eerily similar to the one I had undergone years earlier at Ikeja Police Station. During the interrogation, I was finally informed of the alleged offence that had led to my arrest. According to the officers, my son had reported that I struck him on the head after he returned from school. As I had recounted earlier, he had stood up silently and gone downstairs. Unknown to me, he had returned to his school, where, in a fit of rage, he smashed the sliding glass doors, claiming that I had hit him hard and dangerously in my room. This accusation was the basis for my arrest and detention. I was taken from my house at approximately 17:00 hours. By the time the interrogation was concluded, reports written, DNA samples taken via a saliva swab, fingerprints recorded, and my statement signed, it was nearly 20:00 hours. The DNA and fingerprints were, I assumed, to check whether I was implicated in any other crimes and to update their database. The entire experience was unsettling and surreal.

After completing their procedures, I was escorted into a small room, which contained a single bed with a mattress, a bedsheet, and a pillow, where I was to rest overnight. Throughout the night, no one asked if I wanted food or drink. The only thing I observed was one of the policemen on shift peering through a small open window, covered with burglar bars, to check if I was still breathing and had not harmed myself. I remained in that custody room the entire night–sleepless, confused, and wondering what kind of life I had found myself in. Around 9:00 a.m. the following morning, I was led out of the cell to the reception and informed that I would be released on self-recognition while their investigation continued. Without further explanation, they simply opened the office door and the gate, telling me to leave. Not one of them asked if I had money for transport home, nor did anyone offer to assist me with a lift. At that moment, I concluded that a policeman in a police station, no matter where in the world, is always the same–disconnected from the citizens they are supposed to protect. I believe they were trained to lose their sense of humanity and disregard any compassion for others' welfare. It was only when I stepped outside the police station and onto the main road, which lay around the corner from the building, that I realised I was in the Dagenham East area, a place I was familiar with.

I walked to Dagenham East Station and approached the station attendant, explaining that I had been detained at the police station since the previous day, having been picked up from my home. Now, I was being allowed to return home. I was heading to Becontree Station, just two stops away, but had no money for the journey. The police station offered no support for my return trip from the location where they had arrested me. As is often the case in Britain, the man assessed me carefully, seemingly weighing the truth of my statement and looking for any signs of panic or dishonesty. After a few minutes, he opened the gate and told me to inform the attendant at Becontree Station to contact him if they doubted my story. Upon reaching Becontree Station, I repeated the same explanation and was allowed to leave without further issue. That moment was an act of both compassion and humanity. It marked one of the last times I saw my son. He had been fostered by a Nigerian couple, but I later received troubling reports that he had caused significant trouble by making false accusations about the foster father, nearly getting him jailed with fabricated stories to the social services.

Several years later, I was invited to Barking Magistrates' Court, where my son was facing trial. As a devout Christian, I attended the court on the scheduled day. I recall that two of his sisters, who had never mentioned anything about the case to me, were also present. Just before the case was to be heard, my son informed the social worker accompanying him that he needed to use the toilet. Thirty minutes later, the social services staff came to tell me that my son no longer wanted me to be in the courtroom. He had refused to leave the toilet until I had left the building. Eventually, the presiding magistrate requested that I be brought into the chamber. The judge, apologetically, explained that the boy did not wish for me to be at the hearing. He assured me that he would write a letter to that effect. More than ten years have passed, and I have never received such a letter from the court. In hindsight, it is not something I should lose sleep over. I was later informed that the boy had been fostered by an Asian family. At the time of writing this book, he is 27 years old, with no formal education–no GCSEs, nor any technical qualifications. One of his sisters once mentioned that he now begs for money at Dagenham Heathway Station, sometimes in the evening. What a shameful reflection on my family's reputation.

CHAPTER TWENTY

HOPE AMID DESPAIR

Whatever has a beginning must also have an end. That end may leave us with memories–some pleasant, others less so–to reflect upon or to recall. Yet, an end is an end, just as a beginning will always signify the starting point. Fortunately, despite the bitterness and the harrowing nature of events, my composure, maturity, and the God-given wisdom that the late Bola Ige aptly described as 'wait and see' prevailed. I thank God for granting me the longevity to look back with clarity and recount the stories of my journey through the harrowing experience of detention–a veritable death cage.

Had I struggled with the police at the Aswani Market gate, who knows what might have happened? One of the policemen could have been under some influence, and the outcome might have been fatal. We have read in the newspapers about instances where police, instead of pursuing terrorists or armed robbers, recklessly discharged their firearms under the influence of illicit local gin, popularly known as *ogogoro*, at motor parks or garages. Innocent people have been tragically killed in such incidents. These are often dismissed as *accidental discharges*, with neither apology nor compensation offered to the bereaved families. When the police in Nigeria arrest someone and take them to the station, they often write the individual's statement on their behalf. The person is not afforded the opportunity to read, correct, or contest what has been written; instead, they are forced to sign the document under duress. In my case, I was beaten mercilessly-like a housemaid accused of stealing from her master–subjected to public disgrace and humiliation. My only offence was pleading on behalf of an elderly woman who was being beaten by the officers, a woman old enough to be their grandmother. The value of the plantains she carried on her head would not have been more than ₦150.

When items are confiscated from someone–be it a single shoe or any other possession–due to a suspected offence, protocol dictates that the police should take the items to the station, record them meticulously in their logbook, and await the rightful owner to claim them. To transfer such confiscated items into a private residence constitutes a criminal act, akin to terrorism or armed robbery. In this instance, the robbery was perpetrated by those tasked with upholding the law–the Nigerian police force. The police are expected to bring an individual to the station when they arrest them, request a written report, and ensure it is signed to authenticate the account. However, forcing a detainee out of a vehicle at gunpoint near the station, leaving them in an impoverished state in public view, demonstrates cowardice and a guilty conscience on the part of the officers. Moreover, when a member of the public provides confidential information about someone terrorising their community, the police are entrusted to handle it discreetly. Yet, in Nigeria, it is not uncommon for photocopies of such reports to end up in the hands of the accused, who may then use the information to harm the informant. This betrayal of trust is a significant reason Nigerians cannot trust the Nigerian Police Force.

In contrast, in the United Kingdom, if the identity or address of an informant or whistleblower is leaked, the Metropolitan Police would face serious repercussions. Such a breach would likely result in an investigation by an independent commission, with the police held accountable in court for damages and for endangering the informant's life. This stark difference underscores the gap in accountability and professionalism between the two policing systems. In Nigeria, individuals suspected of offences but not yet found guilty are often detained indefinitely, sometimes for as long as 30 years, with investigations left unresolved. Many detainees lose their sense of worth, reduced to mere shadows of themselves, living yet stripped of their humanity–what I describe as *living skeletons.* Their families, having long assumed them dead, may find that even if these individuals are eventually released, they cannot find their way back home. On the contrary, in the United Kingdom, the situation is markedly different. A person cannot be detained for more than 24 hours without approval from a magistrates' court. While nations, including Nigeria, claim to adhere to United Nations laws and regulations, the reality on the ground often tells a different story.

Reflecting on these differences, I neither encourage nor discourage Nigerians from bringing their spouses or children to the United Kingdom, especially given the prevailing insecurity in Nigeria. However, it is crucial to understand and adapt to the cultural norms here, as they differ significantly from those in Nigeria. For instance, the dynamic of family relationships is vastly different. In Nigeria, men are often seen as the heads of their households, wielding authority over their wives and children. In contrast, in the United Kingdom, the situation is quite the opposite. A man's primary responsibilities are to provide for his family, offer guidance, and nurture their relationship with God. However, when women form friendships here, they may be encouraged to reject rigid rules imposed by their husbands. Similarly, children often find peers who introduce them to social services and law enforcement agencies, which may provide support beyond what their parents can offer. Unfortunately, this sometimes leads to children straying from the values and discipline their parents intended to instil. The Nigerian government must recognise that all human beings, created by God or Allah, deserve to be treated with dignity. This treatment should mirror the compassion and care they hope to receive from God on Earth, in Heaven, or on the Day of Judgement. Arresting people arbitrarily–individuals simply going about their daily work or business–and detaining them indefinitely without due judicial process is inhumane. Innocent people are often coerced into incriminating themselves in cases they know nothing about, lured by false promises of release. Such practices must come to an end if Nigeria is to uphold justice and the rule of law.

No individual detained for any reason–whether for murder, burglary, theft, grievous bodily harm, human trafficking, drug use, or importation–should remain in police custody beyond 24 hours unless the police have obtained a court directive for their continued detention. Imagine a police constable saying to me, 'They learnt you are an influential man in your office and a landlord. If you don't cooperate, we will dump your corpse wherever we please.' Detention facilities, no matter how small, should provide basic necessities: a room with a single bed, a mattress, a bedsheet, and a pillow for each detainee to ensure their dignity and privacy. This responsibility lies with the Minister responsible for police affairs, the Inspector General of Police (IGP), and the Attorney General of the Federation (AGF). It is worth noting that when politicians, bank directors, or the Accountant General of the Federation are arrested for money laundering or embezzlement, they are often granted bail on self-recognition and resolve their cases through out-of-court settlements, refunding only 20% of what they were found to have stolen. Proper nourishment is essential for human health and survival. Yet, serving adult men a meagre two tablespoons of improperly cooked corn and beans at 10 a.m. is effectively a death sentence, accelerating their demise through malnutrition.

Death, as we know, is inevitable. It can claim any parent at any time. My prayer is that God grants the surviving parent the strength and fortitude to provide the children with a proper upbringing–instilling good home values, religious guidance, quality education, and moral behaviour. However, one must not expect all children to conform perfectly to the paths we try to shape for them. Flexibility is key to avoiding conflict with the law, especially in the United Kingdom, where social services often challenge traditional parenting methods inherited from our forefathers. Treat your children as companions and maintain open and respectful communication, recognising them as part of your generation. Finally, make them understand that your struggles are aimed at giving them a better future–one you were not privileged to enjoy during your upbringing. Despite all my efforts to raise my son to be a good and responsible individual, he still refuses to heed my advice. Instead, he listens to his peers, many of whom have no prospects and have become entangled in gang activities.

ABOUT THE AUTHOR

OLATUNJI OLUSANYA is a passionate advocate for justice, human dignity, and societal reform. With a wealth of lived experiences that have shaped his understanding of the challenges within law enforcement and governance, he brings a unique and personal perspective to the conversation about human rights and social equity.

Born and raised in Nigeria, Olatunji Olusanya witnessed firsthand the systemic flaws and injustices that permeate various facets of society, particularly within the criminal justice system. His harrowing experience in police detention–a defining chapter of his life–inspired him to speak out against the inhumane treatment of detainees and the abuse of power by law enforcement agencies. In addition to his advocacy, Olatunji Olusanya is deeply committed to family values, cultural heritage, and the importance of adapting to change. His reflections on raising children across cultural divides–particularly in the UK–offer invaluable insights into navigating the complexities of parenting in an ever-evolving world.

Through his writing, Olatunji Olusanya aims to shed light on critical issues, provoke thought, and inspire action towards

ABOUT THE AUTHOR

creating a more just and equitable society. This book is a testament to his resilience, faith, and unwavering belief in the power of storytelling to drive change.

Olatunji Olusanya currently resides in the United Kingdom, where he continues to engage in social commentary, community advocacy, and mentorship, sharing his life's lessons to empower others.

www.ingramcontent.com/pod-product-compliance
Lightning Source LLC
LaVergne TN
LVHW010223070526
838199LV00062B/4705